THE SPIRITUAL JOURNEY

Anne Bancroft is a former lecturer in Comparative Religion. She has made a number of broadcasts on religious themes on both television and radio, and is a well-known and respected author with a number of highly successful titles to her credit, including *Origins of the Sacred* and *Weavers of Wisdom*.

The Spiritual Journey

ANNE BANCROFT

ELEMENT

Shaftesbury, Dorset ● Rockport, Massachusetts

Published in Great Britain in 1991 by
Element Books Limited
Longmead, Shaftesbury, Dorset

Published in the USA in 1991 by
Element, Inc
42 Broadway, Rockport, MA 01966

Cover painting: St Prolopius the Blessed by Nicholas Roerich
Courtesy of the Nicholas Roerich Museum, New York.
Cover design by Max Fairbrother and Barbara McGavin
Designed by Roger Lightfoot
Typeset by Photoprint, Torquay, Devon
Printed and bound in Great Britain by
Billings Ltd, Hylton Road, Worcester

British Library Cataloguing in Publication Data

A catalogue record for this book is available from the
British Library

Library of Congress Catalog Card Number available

ISBN 1–85230–239–9

Contents

1

The Start of the Journey

AN OLD WOMAN washing her windows, a dog sniffing the hedge, a seagull walking a rooftop – is anything spiritual happening? To the ordinary eye, caught up in the dream we all share of a myself-centred universe, no, nothing spiritual at all, just the same old stuff.

But sometimes curious things occur and it is as though the eye with which we see the world around us changes, as though a new way of looking comes into being. It's not that we suddenly see brilliant technicolour, although occasionally colours do seem stronger. It's more as though a new sense of awareness arises and everything about us is transformed.

This is a phenomenon which puzzles many of us. It is as though something miraculous has occurred, something making itself known which was never there before. It happened to me in my thirties and since then I have always been conscious of the desire to discover more, to make the spiritual journey. Throughout the whole evolving lifetime of humanity, the same transforming event must have occurred and in this book I have described something of what I found out, both about the ways people have responded in the past – and how they are doing so now – and about my own journey.

Perhaps the most wonderful – in the sense of a thing to wonder at – fact in human experience is the constant testimony of people who have known such moments of new vision. They have not always fitted the same name to it but there is evidence from all times and cultures that the same unmistakable clarity has made itself known – often suddenly and unexpectedly and without apparent cause.

To the person who has been given this revelation it seems that there is an inner certainty to be found in everything. All things are so exactly and completely right in themselves that they need no comment or justification – they just are. Life is seen to be without problem; the whole being of the person is so transformed by the perfection and infinite certainty of the experience that there is no word or description apt enough to describe it. There is a timeless simplicity beyond any possible pattern of thinking, which seems to be of the warmest and most wonderful so that the person feels an intense conviction that this is the purpose and fulfilment of living. That insight brings an ecstatic sense of happiness, liberation and lightness, as though one has suddenly woken up in Paradise.

But it is easy to mistake the relief and joy of the experience for the insight itself and to lose the impact of the knowledge that this moment here and now is complete even when there is no ecstasy. We have to learn that ecstasy can come and go but the insight, once experienced, can be discovered again and any moment of clarity may bring it back.

Such insight has nothing to do with being optimistic or thinking oneself to be the possessor of some vast new explanation of the universe. Indeed one feels that explanations fall so short of the mark that they are without any meaning at all. Then, too, there is usually no foreknowledge of the experience before it happens – for instance, it seems often to arise in situations of despair when all alternatives have run out and the only gesture possible is one of complete surrender.

It happened to me in that way when I had reached just such a state, one in which I felt myself entirely to blame. I had come to realize that I was wasting all my years chasing after people and emotional experiences and by doing so I had finally extinguished a sense of spiritual life that I had once known vividly and valued highly. I was deeply remorseful and depressed, believing that I had lost for good something that was infinitely precious.

As a child I had felt that the world about me was full of

wonder and mystery and for a long time had felt that I really belonged to a different dimension of being, one which was filled with a sense of the numinous. But as I grew older I had rejected those feelings completely and instead all the attractions of the social world had taken over and I had turned away from any inner life altogether.

And so, many years later, I came to this time of remorse. I felt that because the rejection had been so complete and all the following years had been so cut off from spiritual life, I must have extinguished that life completely.

One night I could not go to bed, I was feeling deeply sad and repentant. And then when the morning light came and the birds began to sing, I suddenly found myself strangely aware of them. I looked into the garden and saw a blackbird and it was as though I had never seen a blackbird before. It had a significance which was completely new to me and I suddenly felt that this blackbird was the most real thing I had ever seen, and that just to see a blackbird in this way would make life worth living. The days that followed were different from any that had passed before. I was suddenly intensely aware of sound and light and found myself more vulnerable than usual to the impact of other people. Other things – a group of trees, for example – would fleetingly take on the significance of the blackbird. I realized I was coming close to something, some new quality.

One evening I was looking at a branch of rhododendron which I had put in a vase. As I looked, enjoying its beauty but without any purpose in my mind, I began to feel a sense of communication with it, as though it and I had become one. The feeling was immeasurably happy and strong. It came to me then that the whole mystery of existence was not far away from me but very close at hand. And that somehow the secret lay in my relationship with everything about me. That strange sense of oneness with the rhododendron seemed to have come about because I was still, and not wanting anything, and therefore somehow free to see it properly and to know it as itself.

A few days later a new and somehow crowning experience came – and it happened in a most mundane way. It was in the morning and I switched on the wireless to hear a concert. As the first note of music sounded, there was an almost audible click in my mind and I found that everything was transformed. I was in a different state of consciousness altogether. It was as though the separate feeling of 'me' which we all feel had gone, clicked away, and instead there was a great sense of clarity, of utter beneficent wonderful emptiness. And in that emptiness there were no barriers. The stones on the road were exquisitely beautiful and as significant as a person. An upright, old-fashioned bicycle propped by the road was wonderfully funny. It was as though my mind could now embrace, without reserve or judgement, all that it encountered – whether people or animals or things – because it was filled with clearness and emptiness. I was in a state of complete happiness for three days, and then it faded and went.

After it had gone, I decided I must find out everything I could about it. I was not then in the least bit knowledgeable about spiritual life but it seemed to me that what had happened must be in its own way a spiritual experience, although I had never read or heard of anything quite like it. But the effect of that crowning clarity and of those strange weeks of effort and discovery preceding it made me utterly convinced that an unimaginable wonder exists as the essential beingness of everything. And that it exists whether I notice it or not, and that when I do notice it, as I did then, it transforms me. So I knew I could not forget it. I felt somehow as though I was turned round in my mind towards a different direction.

But then I found out that a transformed seeing turns out, in fact, to be a fairly common human experience – it was just that I had never heard of it before. For instance, Marion Milner the psychiatrist says:

One day I was idly watching some gulls as they soared high overhead. I was not interested, for I recognized them as 'just gulls', and vaguely watched first one and then another. Then all at once something seemed to have opened. My idle boredom with the familiar became a deep-breathing peace and delight, and my whole attention was gripped by the pattern and rhythm of their flight, their slow sailing which had become a quiet dance. In trying to observe what had happened I had the

idea that my awareness had somehow widened, that I was
feeling what I saw as well as thinking what I saw.

A Life of One's Own

A widened awareness – that was what I had discovered too
when I looked at the blackbird, the rhododendron, at the
group of trees. Is this, I wondered, the beginning of a
spiritual journey? For those lucky enough to be struck by
wonder, it seems as though it usually is. The experience
echoes on and on and they can never be quite the same again.
But there are also many who never seem to have this
particular sight of the numinous and yet they too come to a
time when they sense there is something vital missing from
their lives. They may not know what it is but they feel it is
there somewhere and without it they are incomplete.

This longing nostalgia is for them the threshold of the
spiritual journey. The acknowledgement that there is something else, a mystery, the mystery of existence itself, is the
key which opens the door for all of us. But such an
acknowledgement is not easy. A fish darting through water
is unlikely to be aware of the water as separate from itself.
We are not usually aware – and may never become aware – of
the spiritual medium in which we live our lives until we
wake up to it.

For that mystery – of our own being and of the meaning of
the universe – has to be experienced rather than understood
and this is where the difficulty lies. Reason and intellect are
our precious tools for life and we know of no other; but the
ultimate meaning of existence has always escaped human
attempts to define it by those tools and it is only when they
are put down and we become open to the unknown, to that
which is unmediated by our discriminating thought, that the
mystery can be felt and the spiritual journey get under way.

And the mystery itself sometimes seems to take a hand at
this point. It pulls us on and if we just want to stay stuck it
won't let us. We come to recognize its ineffable presence as a
different facet of reality, a new way in which the ultimate is
compelling us towards itself. We are obeying an imperative
need.

I fled Him, down the nights and down the days;
I fled Him, down the arches of the years;
I fled Him, down the labyrinthine ways
Of my own mind; and in the midst of tears
I hid from Him, and under running laughter.
Up vistaed hopes, I sped;
And shot, precipitated,
Adown Titanic glooms of chasmèd fears,
From those strong feet that followed, followed after.
                    Francis Thompson, *The Hound of Heaven*

This may be an over-dramatic rendering of the subtle change of direction we begin to experience, but it expresses the sense of inevitability which the new consciousness awakens. It is as though one is going home, and to a home that is somehow infinitely greater than anything the imagination could envisage.

Such a feeling may arise as the result of a personal crisis – as mine did – or when emotions seem to cage us in like prison walls. Such an emotional caging happened to me once when I was young and in love and seemed to have been rejected. I was very unhappy, but one afternoon as I was walking across a field, I suddenly became aware of the shape of the hills ahead of me. I stopped walking and looked at them and as I did so the burden of unhappiness, self-pity and self-absorption seemed to be lifted right out of my mind. I was aware of those hills as I had not been aware of any real thing for a long time and it was a foretaste of my later change of consciousness.

That sort of experience came before I felt any need for a spiritual journey. But others who have discovered the spiritual have recognized its compelling force immediately. Flora Courtois, author of *An Experience of Enlightenment*, says:

The small pale green desk at which I'd been so thoughtlessly gazing had totally and radically changed. It appeared now with a clarity, a depth of three-dimensionality, a freshness I had never imagined possible. At the same time, in a way that is utterly indescribable, all my questions and doubts were gone as effortlessly as chaff in the wind. I knew everything and all at once, yet not in the sense that I had ever known anything before.

This new kind of knowing was so pure and unadorned, so delicate, that nothing in the language of my past could express it. Neither sense nor feeling nor imagination contained it yet all were contained in it. In some indefinable way I knew with absolute certainty the changeless unity and harmony in charge of the universe and the inseparability of all seeming opposites.

She tells us that her quest for reality had begun as a girl in her teens many years ago and it had started with a vision of light.

Only recently have I realized how deeply that vision affected the course of my life right up to this moment. . . . No longer living in the old way, we are lived. Nothing has been lost. All our skills, strategies, relationships and memories are available for service to a more harmonious mode of being.

An Experience of Enlightenment

Douglas Harding, too, author of *On Having No Head*, found his life was changed all at once. The experience happened when he was walking in the Himalayas during the Second World War.

What actually happened was something absurdly simple and unspectacular: just for the moment I stopped thinking. Reason and imagination and all mental chatter died down. For once, words really failed me. I forgot my name, my humanness, my thingness, all that could be called me or mine. Past and future dropped away. It was as if I had been born that instant, brand new, mindless, innocent of all memories. There existed only the Now, that present moment and what was clearly given in it. To look was enough. And what I found was khaki trouserlegs terminating downwards in a pair of brown shoes, khaki sleeves terminating sideways in a pair of pink hands, and a khaki shirtfront terminating upwards in – absolutely nothing whatever! Certainly not a head.

It took me no time at all to notice that this nothing, this hole where a head should have been, was no ordinary vacancy, no mere nothing. On the contrary, it was very much occupied. It was a vast emptiness vastly filled, a nothing that found room for everything – room for grass, trees, shadowy distant hills, and far above them snowpeaks like a row of angular clouds riding the blue sky. I had lost a head and gained a world.

On Having No Head

From then on, headlessness came to be the centre of his life and the magnetic pull of the state caused him to devote all his time to exploring it, teaching it and writing about it.

The authors of classical, definitive works on mysticism such as Evelyn Underhill and William James can add a structure, a groundwork to such experiences and help us to understand the perspectives of the spiritual journey. Evelyn Underhill, author of *Mysticism*, says: 'We are face to face with the "wonder of wonders" – that most real, yet most mysterious of all the experiences of religion, the union of the human and divine, in a nameless *something* . . . it is here that the mystic encounters Absolute Being.'

She outlines three factors underlying that encounter:

1. The unchanging light of Eternal Reality: that Pure Being 'which ever shines and naught shall ever dim'.
2. The web of illusion, here thick, there thin; which hems in, confuses, and allures the sentient self.
3. That self, always changing, moving, struggling – always, in fact, *becoming* – alive in every fibre, related at once to the unreal and to the real; and with its growth in true being, ever more conscious of the contrast between them.

Mysticism

William James, author of *The Varieties of Religious Experience*, suggests four characteristics of spirituality. The first is 'ineffability'. The ineffable is that state of being which defies expression because it goes beyond words. Language – particularly, it seems to me, the English language – has a very small vocabulary for any state in the least uncommon. But fortunately language is not the most important thing because the experience of the ineffable is direct and immediate and is more like a perception or feeling than anything to do with the discriminating intellect. The Greek writer Plotinus says that we will be struck with wonder if we apprehend the ineffable: 'By directing your glance towards it, by reaching it, by resting in it, you will achieve a deep and immediate awareness of it and will at the same time seize its greatness in all things that come from it and exist through it.'

So ineffability is a beyond-words state to be reached and then rested in – similar, perhaps, to the sense of wonder I had experienced with the rhododendron. Earlier this century,

Paul Tillich used a term 'the Ground of Being' which many people found evocative of just that state. The Ground of Being suggests that we are already there, already resting, that the ground is the Ground of our own nature and that our nature is pure being. Such a term helps us to identify ourselves with consciousness and the awakened state.

William James's next characteristic is the noetic, a new insight and knowledge, as though one has discovered truths beyond the reach of the ordinary mind. James says:

> They are states of insight into depths unplumbed by the discursive intellect. They are illuminations, revelations, full of significance and importance, all inarticulate as they remain; and as a rule they carry with them a curious sense of authority for aftertime.
>
> *The Varieties of Religious Experience*

The noetic is the land of the sages: of those, such as Martin Buber whose noetic insight caused him to see that the human personality, what we think of as 'I', exists according to what it is identified with. When it is identified with the body and bodily feelings then it seems to be mortal, fragile and changing. But when it is identified with the Unconditioned, with the Absolute Void, the Godhead, Suchness, or Ground of Being, the 'I' feels changeless and at one with all things.

Such knowledge can only be arrived at by actual experience of the Ground and James's third characteristic is indeed concerned with such experience. He calls it 'transiency' and points out that most mystical states do not last for long, but they can recur and with recognition our experience of them becomes finer. The widened consciousness with which Marion Milner observed the seagulls, for instance, became for her the means by which she found new awareness, an awareness which she could encourage by learning its conditions. Then, as James points out, 'from one recurrence to another it [the spiritual experience] is susceptible of continuous development in what is felt as inner richness and importance.'

Perhaps it is the amount of importance we attach to the mystical experience that is the basic condition for its recurrence. For some people a moment of wonder and unusual clarity is quite easily forgotten and horizontal life resumed as though it had never taken place. For others, it illuminates their everyday living with sublime light and becomes a reference point for all experience.

For Douglas Harding, losing his head brought him to realize that:

> . . . it felt like a sudden waking from the sleep of ordinary life, an end to dreaming. It was self-luminous reality for once swept clean of all obscuring mind. . . . It was a lucid moment in a confused life-history. It was a ceasing to ignore something which (since early childhood at any rate) I had always been too busy or too clever or too scared to see.
>
> *On Having No Head*

For him it was essential to repeat the experience, its importance was so great, and by experimentation he found his own ways of doing so which are well documented in his books.

James's fourth characteristic is passivity. He explains it in this way:

> Although the oncoming of mystical states may be facilitated by preliminary voluntary operations, as by fixing the attention, or going through certain bodily performances, or in other ways which manuals of mysticism prescribe; yet when the characteristic sort of consciousness once has set in, the mystic feels as if his own will power were in abeyance, and indeed sometimes as if he were grasped and held by a superior power.
>
> *The Varieties of Religious Experience*

The apprehension of such a power is perhaps the greatest wonder of the spiritual state and gives the person the confidence of knowing forevermore that there exists a Transcendent, a Reality, and that its dimensions are without limit. If one already believes in God, it is the affirmation of one's belief; if agnostic, it is the unforeseen evidence which shifts the balance of one's understanding; if atheistic, it causes a vast turnaround in attitudes and perceptions, a fundamental reorientation of direction.

The poet Alfred Tennyson discovered the transcendent when he was a boy and had set his own will into abeyance:

A kind of waking trance I have frequently had quite up from boyhood, when I have been all alone. This has generally come upon me through repeating my own name two or three times to myself silently, till all at once, as it were out of the intensity of the consciousness of individuality, the individuality itself seemed to dissolve and fade away into boundless being, and this not a confused state but the clearest of the clearest, the surest of the surest, the weirdest of the weirdest, utterly beyond words, where death was an almost laughable impossibility, the loss of personality (if so it were) seeming no extinction but the true life.

Tennyson: A Memoir

And Bernard Berenson, in his *Sketch for a Self-Portrait*, gives a very simple yet telling example of it when he describes his own moment of radiance:

It was a morning in early summer. A silver haze shimmered and trembled over the lime trees. The air was laden with their fragrance. The temperature was like a caress. I remember – I need not recall – that I climbed up a tree stump and felt suddenly immersed in Itness. I did not call it by that name. I had no need for words. It and I were one.

It seems to me that there are two ways of approaching the spiritual journey. They can be described – very simply – as from the outside inwards and from the inside outwards. Starting from the outside and going inwards is the more traditional way and the one adopted by most religions. Before turning to the inner life, so they maintain, the outer life has to be put in order. The person has to become *moral* first. The Buddha stated it clearly – 'Cease to do evil; learn to do good; purify your own mind.'

A paring away at one's self-indulgent way of life obviously needs to take place at some point and the religions see it as the first step. In Christianity it is called the purgative way. Evelyn Underhill says:

We see a sham world because we live a sham life. We do not know ourselves; hence do not know the true character of our senses and instincts; hence attribute wrong values to their suggestions and declarations concerning our relation to the external world. That world, which we have distorted by identifying it with our own self-regarding arrangements of its elements, has got to reassume for us the character of Reality, of God. . . . Primarily, then, the soul must be purged of all that stands between itself and goodness: putting on the character of reality instead of the character of illusion or 'sin'.

Mysticism

So in mystical Christianity and also in Buddhism moral discipline is the essential preliminary. Five precepts are taken in Buddhism and then meditated on. The process is a psychological and slow one; many years may be spent studying the mental turmoils that, hitherto repressed, now make themselves known during meditation. To cease to do evil is not enough, it is necessary to learn to do good; and purification of the mind through examination and observation, quietening and stilling – however long it takes – is seen as the best way to accomplish it.

The other path of the spiritual journey, going from inside to out, follows the advice given by the Indian sage, Ramana Maharshi – 'To inhere in the Self is the thing. Never mind the mind.' This is the way taken by those who, either because the suffering of feeling themselves barren and without grace is intolerable, or through having received an illuminative insight, feel such a longing for the Infinite that their need is for surrender to its splendour and to live from that liberated state forevermore. Penetrating to the core is all they want to do and the long years of self-examination and training in morality seem to bear little resemblance to their goal. 'Once the core is grasped, everything else will become relatively insignificant and crystal clear,' says the Chinese master, Chang Chen Chi; and Meister Eckhart advises: 'Up then, noble soul! Put on your jumping shoes which are intellect and love, and overleap the worship of your mental powers, overleap your understanding and spring into the heart of God.'

The traditionalists see such leaps without enthusiasm. They say, perhaps with some justification, that 'instant enlightenment' without a thorough knowledge of the self will lead to delusion and waste, that it is essential to be grounded before you take to the air.

Those who have received illumination, however, often

find that moral obligations and responsibilities *follow* their insight and that turning to the outer world from an inner certainty makes all the ensuing work on the self both inevitable and right. Inevitable because the person feels so different spiritually that there is no possibility of the old self staying unaltered; and right because there is a new integration which warns against attempts to make a *perfect* outer self, to attempt to manipulate in order to satisfy an ideal.

The traditionalists are wary of insights, seeing them as ephemeral rockets that leave no trace; the mystics are impatient with traditional methods, seeing these as a spiritual technology tinkering with the mechanics of enlightenment but missing the essence of it.

Some religious practices manage fairly successfully to combine the two. One is Zen Buddhism, which fully acknowledges the luminous experience but suggests that the real work starts afterwards, when the results must be put to use to benefit the world. So Zen practitioners, at least in theory, aim to live highly disciplined lives both before and after enlightenment.

> Only when you have no thing in your mind and no mind in things are you vacant and spiritual, empty and marvellous.
> Lien-teng Hui-yao in *Essays in Zen Buddhism*

In this book, the direction I have taken is towards the inside out rather than the outside in. Hence there are few descriptions of traditional methods for reaching realization. But in later chapters there are descriptions of some of the ways that have worked for me in my own continuing journey towards that state.

2

The First
Journeyers

FOR SOME YEARS I lived in south Dorset, in a quiet, rather mysterious countryside of little winding lanes that seemed to have no end and high rounded hills that often bore traces of a previous civilization on their summits. This is the country of stone circles standing within small untrodden woods, of mounds sometimes a hundred metres long containing passage graves, of earthen circles within circles and of vast hilltop earthworks, such as Maiden Castle, which took several million human work hours to build.

It was impossible to drive for even a short distance without seeing some evidence of the people who had lived there thousands of years ago and as time went by I felt the urge to find out all I could and in some way to make contact with those other spiritual travellers who had left such compelling religious landmarks.

And then I was drawn even further back in time by a visit to Kent's Cavern, an immense cave with thousands of metres of passage and gallery, some of which now have electric light. There are great chambers of multicoloured rock, mainly the red of iron and green of copper, showing a glowing beauty undreamed of when one stands outside. Nothing feels inimical or hostile in the warmth of the cave. It is at the same time both majestic and intimate. So it was not difficult to imagine such a place, consistently mild and excellently ventilated, as a cosy home to many stray creatures, including some of the earliest humans – and there is evidence of their presence there 300,000 years ago.

For those early men and women, heightened perception of their background – of the mountains and rivers and the sea – would probably have formed their basic sense of religion. They were not likely to have stood apart from the environment in the way we do today. Like the trees of the forest they were as they were, and their sense of spirituality would have come (as it still does to many mystics) from their openness to what was there – the streams bubbling up through the ground, the curve of the hills, the clouds.

For an immense aeon these people lived in a timeless world – we know this because they went on using the same primitive stone tools for some 400,000 years. In this timeless 'dream' period they probably felt themselves very much in the present, as animals seem to. They would have been open and alert and unlikely to have felt the desire for 'things' that modern humanity does. Indeed, we might have found them no more primitive than ourselves in their morals and modes of thought, for the ability to be technically brilliant is not the final measure of culture and goodness.

Much nearer to our own time – although still cave dwellers – were the artists who etched the rock paintings in the great French caves of Lascaux, Trois Frères and others. These magnificent etched paintings present us with clear evidence of the seriousness and passion felt for the sacred by the humans of thirty thousand years ago. Most of the paintings are of animals, but these portrayals are more than just trophies of the hunt, they are animals felt in all their animal totality, their beingness. Life and movement is captured in just a few vivid lines – a high-maned wild horse with neck stretched and legs in flight, a slow clumsy bear ambling along, a lion, full-faced, staring out at the onlooker, the round eyes of a mammoth. The Ice Age artists discovered the spiritual presence within the reality, timelessness within time, and the emotion which moved them has made these paintings unforgettable for us.

They were sacramental paintings and this is shown by the fact they they were undertaken far within the dark interiors, down winding passages and on walls that seem almost inaccessible even today with modern cave equipment. There are plenty of smooth and easy-to-reach walls near cave entrances but they were left untouched. It was in the most unreachable overhangs and recesses that the men and women painted. They must have had to lie on their backs and use long rods, or even work doubled up. They cut on the rock face by means of stone knives. They probably used lamps made of grease-soaked moss which could only have cast a feeble and flickering light.

The greatest spiritual dedication inspired their work and we know that the powerful symbiosis between human and animal and all the living world was the basis of their religious understanding. The shaman was their mediator. He was the manifest bridge between their commonly experienced world and all others. He was the incarnate link bringing animal spirit and human together; and the greatest cave picture of all is of the shaman himself.

In his book *The Rock Pictures of Europe*, Herbert Kuhn relates how he was taken to an almost inaccessible cavern, first gliding on a small skiff along a subterranean river and then creeping and worming his way through nearly impassable passages. The first hall he reached was full of sculptured rock bisons. Around the sculptures the clay floor had hardened with time to the texture of stone, holding within it the footprints of Ice Age people. Their heel marks had been pressed into the ground, indicating that a circular dance had taken place – perhaps a bison dance to ensure the increase of herds, although another explanation could be that initiation ceremonies took place in this hall.

At the far end of the sanctuary, poised in a dancing movement with his head turned to face the onlooker, was the great 'Sorcerer of Trois Frères', the shaman himself, the earliest known depiction of a human being. Kuhn tells us:

An eerie thrilling picture, with his large dark eyes he gazes at the visitor. It is impressive, it is even alarming to look steadily into those eyes which for millennia have stared down from a height into vacant space. This shaman wears upon his head the mask of a stag with its antlers. Bear's paws cover the hands and a horse's tail hangs from his waist. One leg is raised in a dance.

The Rock Pictures of Europe

Perhaps to emphasize the shaman's magic powers there are drawings in the same cave of three strangely portrayed figures. One has a man's legs, a horse's tail, a bison's head, and the front two legs of an animal with one hoof cloven. He seems to be dancing and accompanying himself with music on a bowed instrument. In front of him is a female animal, half deer and half bison. The dancing figure appears to be charming her with his music for the great bison head is turned towards him. Leading the little group is a reindeer whose forelegs end in long human fingers. Here is animal magic indeed.

What is a shaman? We now have a good deal more knowledge than was possible some years ago, for recently shamanism has excited considerable interest worldwide and much study has been made of it in present primitive societies, particularly those of Mongolia, North America and Australia. We know that with the help of his tribe, who are beating drums and chanting, the shaman – often clothed in the guise of a particular animal or bird – goes into a trance during which he is said to perform miraculous deeds, communicating with the dead, with animals and birds, and reaching a state which is believed to transcend the usual human one. He is looking for a primordial consciousness of purity and innocence. Shamanistic societies almost always believe in a lost paradise, a time when heaven and earth were one, when humans could talk to the gods and animals, when the world had complete access to itself with one shared language for all creatures.

The shaman's trance and ecstasy are meant to re-enact that prefallen state. It is believed that he transcends the time barrier – the existence of time being thought of as a consequence of the 'fall'. Nowadays he ascends out of time in his 'spirit', whereas it is said that he once did so in the flesh. It is believed that his spirit passes from his body and travels on exotic journeys through other realms. He can bring back the wandering spirit of the person who is ill and restore him to his body; go with the souls of the dead to their next existence; appeal to the gods for their mercy on the spirit of a sacrificed animal.

In Ice Age times it would have been communication with animals which mattered more than anything. We know that nowadays, in present shamanistic communities, the shaman encounters an animal at some point during his initiation and that this animal becomes his constant (although invisible to others) companion and teaches him animal language. Such a creature's presence seems to reach straight back to those far-off days of the Ice Age when bear, bison, lion, reindeer and mammoth were venerated for their spirit and strength. Such veneration is never seen as a regression to an inferior level. Rather, the ability to speak the language of the great animals and to enter their life is believed to enhance the human soul by much richness of experience.

Before he sets out on his spirit journey, the shaman must perform the act of 'recovery' of animal friendship – he must restore the prefall unity which animal and man shared. No cosmic journey can take place until he has attained to a state of purity, often accomplished through ascetic practices and meditation. Then, it is thought, he will be clear enough to experience ecstasy and thus be able to act spontaneously and with true effect. Such abilities are not obtainable in the ordinary world. Consequently, in order to go to other worlds, he masks and dresses himself as an animal and imitates animal behaviour. The animal he calls back to life is his other self and when it enters him during the trance he changes into this mythical animal companion (often thought of as the ancestor of the tribe).

This is our own religious inheritance, regardless of our race or nationality, for people of the Ice Age migrated to every part of the world. The human spiritual journey has deep roots, deeper by far than the Ice Age, but it is to that extraordinary time that we can trace at least some of our inheritance.

What has the shaman and his animal identity to do with us now? Shamanistic feelings may lurk somewhere in our genes but do they really affect our own spirital journey? For many people the answer is, yes. To believe in the existence of a soul which passes out of the body; in reincarnation; in bread turned into divine flesh and wine turned into holy blood by a divinely ordained priest, is to believe in a certain form of religious magic. It works. It gives the recipient at the communion rail a particular feeling of blessedness, a sense of other worlds apart from the mundane, a feeling of sanctity.

Should we ask for anything more? I think we should. Our own spiritual journey may encompass the shaman-priest if we want it to, but in the end he has to be left behind. Some may prefer to bypass him altogether. Nicholas Berdyaev once said:

> Mysticism is union with God, magic with the spirits of nature . . . Mysticism is the sphere of liberty, magic of necessity. Mysticism is detached and contemplative, magic is active and militant; it reveals the secret forces of humanity and of the world without being able to reach the depths of their divine origin. Mystical experience constitutes precisely a spiritual deliverance from the magic of the natural world, for we are fettered to this magic without always recognizing it.
>
> *Freedom and Spirit*

The division between mysticism and magic is perhaps more fluid than Berdyaev allows and not so definite. But Evelyn Underhill, a true mystic, was equally severe on magic. She says that magic is presented as a pathway to reality but that this is a promise which cannot be fulfilled, for merely to change phenomena does not lead to unity with the Absolute.

> Magic even at its best extends rather than escapes the boundaries of the phenomenal world. It stands, where genuine, for that form of transcendentalism which does abnormal things, but does not lead anywhere: and we are likely to fall victims to some kind of magic the moment that the declaration 'I want to know' ousts the declaration 'I want to be' from the chief place in our consciousness.
>
> *Mysticism*

Knowledge of shamanistic religion was not widespread when she wrote about magic, but she was aware of its long history, calling it a 'great and ancient tradition' and saying:

> Its laws and the ceremonial rites which express those laws, have come down from immemorial antiquity. They appear to enshrine a certain definite knowledge and a large number of less definite theories, concerning the sensual and supersensual worlds, and concerning powers which man, according to occult thinkers, may develop if he will.
>
> *Ibid*

The shaman certainly developed those powers and he lives within us all at an unconscious level. Thus there comes a point in our spiritual journey when we have to consider and assess our own beliefs and reactions to magic. What is the motive, for instance, for belonging to a religion? Is it out of fear – fear of what will happen to us if we don't take part in certain ceremonies and rituals which may contain powerful magic, or if we don't believe in the doctrines? Fear is the dark side of religion. Love is the light side, a love which sees the wonder of the world as it is, in all its ordinariness, and has no wish to change or manipulate it. When the painters Gauguin and van Gogh lived together for a time, Gauguin was constantly irritated by van Gogh's paintings, which were simply of what he saw. Why don't you use your imagination, he would ask, and van Gogh would reply in wonderment, but what imagined thing could be better than the reality of the old olive tree, the cypress on the hill, the iris blossom? The mystic Simone Weil would have agreed with him, as she too saw the full recognition of all that exists as a form of prayer.

But we should not lose sight of the positive side of the shaman's powers out of a high-minded disdain for magic. In ancient times the shaman was the one who healed and brought to life and there is a deeply-rooted instinct in most of us that longs to do the same. So we should not reject the shaman but ask instead what there is of positive spiritual significance that we can learn. The first thing that springs to mind is entering the world of animals, which means changing our stereotyped world view.

It is not so very long ago that we in this country revered the innocent strength of animals. During the centuries immediately before the birth of Christ and for a little while afterwards, the gods of Europe were often portrayed in animal form – hoofed gods, wild boar gods, and antlered deer gods. Their statues, adorned with sculpted gold neckrings, have survived to this day. The horse-goddess Epona continued to be worshipped by the Romans in the north of Britain until at least the second century AD.

If we are to attempt that shamanistic journey into the 'feel' of animal life we need a new openness to our surroundings.

We need to pay attention. When Marion Milner was watching seagulls (Chapter 1) she found she was paying a different kind of attention to them than she normally did and she entered their world in a new way.

We need to change the boundaries of our tight existence by looking at things and listening to them in a way that leaves the self free. Listening is as important as looking. If we go close to a tree and with full attention just listen to it, we may get a sense of what treeness is. It is a question of being still within and open so that the feeling of the tree, or the dog on the corner, or the grass growing can make itself known. In this way we extend our boundaries and enter new worlds and, most important of all, we begin to feel a relationship with all that is.

The real virtue of the shaman lies most of all in the relationship with living things he shared with his followers. He helped them to extend their identity, to be the river and also the fish they caught, the forest and the animal they hunted. They felt reverence for every object in their surroundings in a way we have forgotten, but which we need to remind ourselves of as often as we can. Interexistence seems to be no longer essential to our lives but we suffer if we lose our sense of it. The Iroquois Indian, Rarihokivats, said: 'If you just say "I am part of the universe" then it is possible for you to withdraw from the universe at some point and set up your own separate shop. On the other hand if the universe is part of you, and not only just a part that can be amputated, but a part upon which you are dependent, then you cannot separate yourself, you cannot withdraw.' We need to let the universe in.

As much an essential of our inherited humanity as the magic of the shaman, is the desire we have to worship. The shaman is the journeyer to the land of the gods but he is not the god in person. From archaeological discoveries we find objects of worship that date back some 60,000 years when Homo sapiens, the true human, was not long on the scene. These objects are small statuettes of women. The first to be found was carved out of mammoth tusk and was wonderfully stylized to give emphasis to great buttocks and heavy breasts. It was thought that this was some erotic figure signifying a fertility cult, but since that first discovery more than 130 of these female figures have been found and many are slim, without any particular bodily characteristics. They have graceful heads (a French one wears a cap) and several have been found placed in shrines, so it is now certain they were religious objects. They seem to point to a worship of the female body as being itself the focus of divinity. These 'Venus' figurines, as they were called, continued to be made throughout many thousands of years up to the end of the Stone Age, and consequently they are thought of as representing 'the Great Mother'. Historians now believe that the Great Mother represented bodily existence, nature, water and earth, and also life and death, and that it was worship of her that inspired humanity throughout a vast aeon of time.

Study of the Great Mother has now intensified with pressure from the women's movement and within the last few years much more has been discovered by examining the 5,000-year-old rock carvings of Brittany, Ireland and Malta, caves covered with remarkable carved spirals and patterns of lines. Ken Wilber, in his book *Up From Eden*, draws attention to the emergence of the Great Goddess from the Great Mother. He says that the Great Goddess represented the 'initial insights into a truly transcendental Oneness, a Oneness that is not simply the naturic background of the Great Mother or Earth Mother, but rather the one Form and Divine Ground of all space and time.' Historians who have studied the rock patterns agree in the main that they point to a worship of the Goddess and that this is widespread in the world.

If, then, we could sum up the early spiritual experience of humankind we could say that of the first importance was the earth itself. It was sacred in itself and it manifested a multitude of equally sacred forms – rocks, trees, water, shadows, animals. Each object, however insignificant, revealed the nature and reality of the whole, hence the reverence and also the guilt for that which had to be taken for food. And hence, too, the feeling that the earth was a mighty womb which gave birth to the whole of creation. The earth itself, immanent with Being, was undoubtedly the earliest spirituality known to humankind.

As time passed, the growth of settled agricultural communities began. Then the Earth Mother receded in popular belief and her place was taken by the Great Goddess. She came to be represented by a multitude of hunting and fertility goddesses. They were not the manifestations of the cosmos, as was the Earth Mother – their roles were less mighty, but clearer and more dramatic.

When the nomadic hunters were absorbed into farming communities a whole revolution in the way people thought about time took place. Time became cyclical. And as agriculture grew to be the main means of livelihood the identification with animals – that strange and mystical symbiosis of the Ice Age – was replaced by what the anthropologist Mircea Eliade calls 'the mystical solidarity between man and vegetation'. This led to the great earthworks and mysterious stone circles of the next age, the age that I began this chapter with.

Eliade believes that those earthworks were built to portray the rhythm of fecundity, for the passage graves buried deep within the mounds resemble in their formation the womb and the passage to it. The death and rebirth every year of the earth is probably the major reason for the extraordinary accuracy with which the entrances were aligned to the sun and the moon at the solstices of the year.

That the sun divinity was masculine is very likely, although belief in the masculinity of the sun is less widespread than in the femininity of the moon. The earth receives fertilizing semen-rain from above (Eliade points out that women in Australia and Africa still lie in the rain when they want to conceive) and the sun with its phallic rays is the organ which brings forth plants from the ground. At an even deeper level of consciousness, the darkness of the earth is related to unknown depths of feeling, to sexual responses, to the womb, to the night, whereas the light of the sun is related to conscious life, to individual ambition such as that of kings (who have often taken the sign of the sun as their own). The most ancient gender symbol of all, the Chinese yang and yin, shows masculine as white and feminine as black.

Accompanying the Great Goddess into this age of earth temples came her symbols, which have been found in many places – the carved bird, the serpent, the polished double-axe which represents her fertility and also the ox-horns of the fertile moon-earth Mother. Sacred pillars and trees are associated with her, wild animals follow her and horned beasts were sacrificed to her. She, the Mother/Goddess, has been the longest continuous spiritual idea in humanity's history and worship of her continues in many places to this day, where we know her under the name of Mary or Kali or Tara or Kuan Yin.

In my own pursuit of stone circles and earth temples, I became particularly aware of Avebury in Wiltshire, one of the greatest temples of them all. Even more than Stonehenge, I found it mysterious and amazing and have been drawn back to it again and again.

It is the largest of the 900 stone circles in Britain. It once contained a hundred huge sarsen stones but only some of them remain for much of Avebury was destroyed in the eighteenth century by both the Church (who could not tolerate anything 'pagan') and by a local farmer, 'Stonekiller' Robinson, who hired gangs of men to smash and burn the stones. Enough is left, though, to make it a 'cathedral' of the late Stone Age.

Avebury is an exceptionally serene and beautiful place, full of nuances of rising and falling ground, shadows from the great stones, soft high grass-covered embankments and ancient trees, grazing sheep and singing larks. It is a place implicit with being, its subtle strength carrying a true feeling of spirituality to its visitor.

Nearby is Silbury Hill, the largest man-made mound in Europe and at least five thousand years old. This hill, some prehistorians believe, is a representation of the Eye Goddess – an aspect of the Great Goddess.

Michael Dames, in his book *The Silbury Treasure*, has shown through photograph and description that one of the uses of this tiered chalk hill, which has a central cone of exact measurements, was as a solid eye gazing up at the sky. At nearby Durrington Walls, a causewayed earthwork bounded by six concentric circles, the Eye Goddess is shown on pottery discovered there. Eyes made up of concentric circles gaze out from different pots and Dames says that pot and building offer two views of the one reality. He believes that at Silbury '. . . the dark hidden eye was expanded, using concentric and radial chalk walling, to turn the entire hill into a fat treatment of the eye motif, appropriate for harvest.'

A divine female or divine male, sometimes both, has dominated the religious experience of most of us since birth. When we can look at the origins of our conditioning with a detached but sympathetic eye we can see that there are good psychological reasons at the root of this worship, although once the reasons are understood and the psychology accepted there is no need (even though there may be pleasure) in continuing to worship any deities.

The Earth Mother, representing life, death and renewal, is the side of ourselves most linked to the earth itself, to vegetation, to the caring for all that the earth produces, to the feeling of ourselves as being totally of the earth (and of the sky and the moon and the stars) so that, through us, the earth expresses itself. With this acceptance, the Great Mother is satisfied within us all. For she is affirmation of life and if we cannot affirm her – and many cannot for she creates the stink of decay as well as the scents of summer – we remain psychologically handicapped.

The Goddess is the essential female within all of us, man or woman. She is the wonderfully creative sexual energy which extends into almost every aspect of our lives. Essentially she is the purveyor of the gift of creation and to acknowledge oneself as the willing receiver, open and ready, is to be one with the Goddess. Many find this hard to do for it involves a deep surrender to one's own sexuality – not only in the sexual act itself but also in the much broader way of accepting oneself totally as both male and female, without barriers or denials or confusion.

The spiritual journey is towards that which transcends sex and is altogether unknown. But on the way we must not discard too soon the deep secrets of our nature formed by thousands of years when men and women evolved from stooping creatures to perceptive human beings. Like the small tail we still carry at the base of our spines from prehistoric times, they are part of us and when we fully acknowledge them they become tranquil and beneficent helpers in our spiritual growth. And sometimes we can acknowledge them with nostalgia:

> Why should a bird in that solitary hollow,
> Flying from east to west,
> Seem in the silence of the snow-blanched sunshine
> Gilding the valley's crest
> Envoy and symbol of a past within me
> Centuries now at rest?
>
> Walter de la Mare, *The Solitary Bird*

3

The Western Journey

THOSE OF US who grew up in the West have our spiritual roots not only in prehistoric culture but, more recently, in other religions. All that I had learnt about the cave artists, and especially about the circles and tombs in the countryside about me, made me long to know how those religions had evolved, what had happened next. How did those communities who toiled so vigorously to build Stonehenge and Maiden Castle and Avebury and Silbury Hill come to an end? What happened to their spiritual journey and how was it passed on? Would it affect my own or was this all just idle curiosity?

Whatever the motive, I decided I would try to find out more, mainly because I felt there was a stream of true spiritual experience winding down the ages and I wanted to be within it, feel myself a part of it. It seemed the Stone Age had been unusually marked by adoration and worship in a very close-knit, communal way. But when it ended, in the Age of Iron, it looked at first as though some essential value had changed in people's hearts in the same way that sharp metal swords were replacing stone axes. But I decided this was the historian's viewpoint, one which took account of battles rather than contemplation; and as I delved deeper it seemed to me that life might have changed but the spirit was still running true. For during that time, and probably earlier, the Celtic people were emerging all over Europe and were bringing alive once more the ancient love of natural things which is the mark of the mystic.

Celtic culture was what the historian Nora Chadwick calls 'the fine flower of the Iron Age, the last phase of European material and intellectual development before the Mediterranean world spread northwards over the Continent and linked it to the world of today.' It was also perhaps the last great mystical culture and religion of Europe, one which still paid passionate reverence to earth and water, trees and stars. It was a religion of myth and legend, told and retold, forbidden to be written down.

It is often taught that the Romans brought civilization to the West, but in fact the civilization was already there and all they did was adapt it to their own needs. They took many religious ideas from the countries in their empire – from the Egyptians, the Greeks and the Celts. Celtic culture was undoubtedly finer than the native Roman, with a great sense of poetry and legend, and the Romans were baffled by the clever way the Celts expressed themselves in riddles. They were also impressed by the respect given to the bards. Even when the armies were drawn up for battle the Celtic soldiers would be calmed by the bards, who would launch themselves into the thick of the fighting chanting their prayers.

The more I read about the Celts the more I felt my own roots linked to theirs. As a child, my sense of spiritual presence had always taken place near trees and I discovered that the sacred wood was of first importance to the Celts. They gave a mystical meaning to the individual trees and formed their alphabet on the names of trees. Robert Graves tells us that in all Celtic languages *trees* means *letters* and the Druidic colleges were always founded in woods or groves.

The heroes themselves were often identified with trees – 'The high branches of the alder-tree are on your shield. Your name is Bran, of the dazzling branches . . .' But the Celts took delight in interwoven identities, so that Bran as an alder-tree could also be a raven and this meant he was identified with the Celtic god, Lug – and so on. They loved correspondences, one thing corresponding to another, sometimes in startling leaps, and in this way they expressed with joyful mental agility the deep religious feeling that the whole world is interlinked and interrelated. Transformations were natural in this way of looking – heroes underwent transformations from swineherds to crows to sea-monsters to Irish kings. The wizard gods shifted their shape, were invisible at will, manifested under different forms.

What did such magical processes have to do with the spiritual way? It seemed to me that the relationship lay in a sense of identity with all life, both in its material and its transcendent nature. The Celts, like the shamanistic cave-dwellers before them and the megalith builders, saw the continual dance of the two together – the transcendent within the form and the form expressing the transcendent. The material form was never thought to be rigid and autonomous as it is today – never merely a thing or self-created – but always liquid, dancing, filled with the otherness of the spirit. One thing could change into another because nothing was final or completed – all things had infinite potentiality.

Another link with my own feelings was the Celtic Otherworld, where time no longer existed. It was not so much the concept of an actual other world, a paradise, that I felt close to, as to the apprehension that other dimensions existed and that we can sometimes approach them. The Celts believed that many worlds exist simultaneously, circling each other, interpenetrating sometimes in one circumstance or another. The subtle, nebulous area of twilight or dawn, the river's edge, the horizon, were felt to be haunted by the meeting of worlds. At the heart, the centre, of all these worlds was the timeless Otherworld.

But nearest of all to me was the Celtic passion for the nature of a place, for its essence. Enchantment lay for them, as it often had for me particularly as a child, in the deep intense green of woodland and field, in soft beautiful landscape – which still, in Wales or Ireland, can be secret as though, were one to walk far into the shining green woods, a magic would steal over one changing one eternally.

And I came to love the poetry of the Irish Celts, whose use of words was as liquid and beautiful as the trees and water they described:

> You are the lovely red rowan that calms the wrath and anger
> of all men, like a wave of the sea from flood to ebb, like a wave
> of the sea from ebb to flood . . .

Having discovered and revelled in the Celts, I then found
myself puzzled as to how their religion had died out. I knew
of course the historical facts, that they could not stand up
against the Romans and were forced further and further west
into Brittany and Wales and Ireland; and that pockets of them
existed for centuries in Germany, France and England. I
knew about the antagonism between the Roman Catholics
and the Celtic Catholics, only resolved and that superficially
in the seventh century. But there was a big gap somewhere
between the spirit of the Celts whose religion echoed with
joy and beauty, and the sombre desert religion of Christianity,
with its Biblical injunctions of 'Thou shalt not . . .' I found
myself in accord with Joseph Campbell, when he wrote:

> Within a world that is itself divine where God is immanent
> throughout, in the impulse of the flight of birds, the lightning,
> the fall of rain, the fire of the sun, there is an epiphany of
> divinity in all sight, all thought, and all deeds, which – for
> those who recognize it – is a beginning and end in itself. There
> is for all, and with all, a universal revelation. Whereas within a
> world that is not itself divine, but whose Creator is apart, the
> godhead is made known only by special revelation – as on
> Sinai, or in Christ,. or in the words of the Koran; and
> righteousness then consists in placing oneself in accord not
> with nature but with Sinai, with the lesson of Christ or with
> the Koran; and one lives not simply to play the part well that is
> in itself the end, like the grapevine producing grapes, but, as
> Christ has said, 'so that my Father may reward'. The goal is
> not here and now, but somewhere else.
>
> *Occidental Mythology*

Yet even so, Christianity, I thought, must hold the key to the
next step of the spiritual journey because what else had been
allowed to thrive in the West? Somewhere the spirit of
greenness and adoration must have continued, because true
mysticism cannot be narrowed down to church services and
dark church buildings. But how was it expressed? And then I
came across that next stage and realized that no longer would
mysticism be a religion of the people but that from then on it

would be the responsibility of individuals. I found the writings of Hildegarde of Bingen and saw that she had been the next link in the chain.

Hildegarde was born in Germany in 1096 and at the age of eight was sent to be educated by an anchoress, Jutta, who lived in a cell attached to a monastery. She stayed there for many years and in the course of time other women joined them. When Hildegarde was thirty–eight Jutta died and she was appointed to take over the community. Four years later she had a very strong awakening experience – in proper medieval language she describes it as being inflamed by a fiery light – and for the first time she began to write. Her book took ten years and was the great creative work of her life. She called it *Scivias* (Know the Ways) and in it she set forth not only her own understanding but also her paintings which were illuminations of her dreams and visions.

The part of Germany she lived in had held a Celtic community for longer than most places – indeed the founder of the monastery was an Irish Celtic saint, St Disibode. So when I came across Hildegarde I recognized at once the aspect of the spirit I loved – greenness. One of the most important of her words was *viriditas*, usually translated as 'greening power'. No other theologian of the time saw God in that way. She believed that all creation and humanity is 'showered with greening refreshment, the vitality to bear fruit', and she goes on:

> Greening love hastens to the aid of all. With the passion of heavenly yearning, people who breathe this dew produce rich fruit.

She believed that Christ brought 'lush greenness' to 'shrivelled and wilted people' and says: 'the word is all verdant greening, all creativity'. She calls God the purest spring, his creativity bubbling up in all things; and she sees salvation as a healing moistness. 'The soul,' she says, 'is the freshness of the flesh, for the body grows and thrives through it just as the earth becomes fruitful through moisture.' She wrote an opera, Ordo Virtutum, and in it is sung: 'In the beginning all creatures were green and vital; they flourished amidst flowers. Later the green figure itself came down.' Thus she calls Jesus greenness incarnate. In one of her poems she hears God speaking:

> I am the breeze that nurtures all things green.
> I encourage blossoms to flourish with ripening fruits,
> I am the rain coming from the dew,
> That causes the grasses to laugh
> With the joy of life.
>
> *Meditations with Hildegarde of Bingen*

In this way Hildegarde drew attention to the pleasure of natural things, to the joy and wonder of what she called 'co-creating with God'. She saw the whole earth as imbued with the sacred. She wrote: 'O holy spirit, you are the mighty way in which every thing that is in the heavens, on the earth, and under the earth, is penetrated with connectedness, penetrated with relatedness.' The relationship of all things to each other was the essence of theology to her. She said: 'God has arranged all things in the world in consideration of everything else.'

So sin, to her, was not the sins of the flesh, for that is a concept of sin which is surely based on fear of the body and to her the body was holy. She saw real sin as being against greenness, against the earth itself, against God's creation. For the creating of the cosmos in all its materiality had been an act of love:

> Out of the original source of true love in whose knowledge the cosmic wheel rests, there shines forth an exceedingly precise order over all things. And this order which preserves and nourishes everything comes to light in a way that is ever new . . . Love draws to itself all who desire God and with this impulse Love goes to meet them.
>
> *Ibid*

That God was in any sense remote from the world was impossible for her to conceive, for God and his world were one and indivisible and she only had to look about her to be reassured of that fact. And, as well, she only had to practise the most natural and easiest of meditations to be fully conscious of the presence of God. She says:

> In seeing – to recognize the world,
> In hearing – to understand,

In smelling – to discern,
In tasting – to nurture,
In touching – to govern.
In this way humankind comes to know God for God is the
author of all creation.

Ibid

I wondered if Hildegarde was the one and only exception to
the general trend in Christianity of conceiving God as absent
from the world and people born 'fallen'. But I soon
discovered that she had been very influential on future
generations of mystics, such as Eckhart and Ruysbroeck. The
great Meister Eckhart of a century later believed, as she had
done, that the world was permeated by the divine. Eckhart
said:

> When is a man in mere understanding? I answer, 'When a man
> sees one thing separated from another.' And when is a man
> above mere understanding? That I can tell you: 'When a man
> sees All in all, then a man stands beyond mere understanding.'
>
> *Meister Eckhart*

In his day the Church believed that man was the greatest of
God's creatures and everything else was without soul. He
challenged this view, as Hildegarde would have done:

> God gives to everything alike, and as flowing forth from God
> things are all equal; angels, man and creatures all proceed from
> God alike in their first emanation . . . if here in time they are
> alike, in timelessness they are much more so. Any flea as it is in
> God is nobler than the highest of angels is in himself. Things
> are all the same in God: they are God himself.
>
> *Ibid*

It was for such pronouncements as these that he was accused
of heresy and summoned to appear before the Inquisition. He
was confined in Avignon but died before the trial took place.

The medieval mystics were the ones, then, who gave voice
to the sacred nature of all existence. And they did so against a
background of blood and war, rebellions, persecutions and
plagues. Not only were their emperors at war but so too
were the small princes, dukes and nobles. In many areas the
countryside was laid waste and those who did not die by the
sword perished of starvation or plague. The Church, intent

only on its internal power struggles, provided little in the way of help or consolation, and slid further and further into a morass of immorality and corruption.

In spite of such horrors, the mystics of Germany and the Low Countries, while never shunning the strife around them, yet concentrated on the inner life and so were able to bring perspective and balance into the hearts of all who listened to them. But marvellous as I found their teachings, it was the English ones that seemed to me to echo Hildegarde's sacred greenness most closely.

England did not suffer quite such agonies and storms as swept through central Europe and its mysticism has a somewhat different feel. It is simple, direct, vital. In spite of the Black Death, in spite of the brutish cruelty still to be found at all levels, and the dirt and poverty, medieval England was still Merrie England. The historians picture it as colourful, hardy and joyous.

In the fourteenth century Julian of Norwich, like Hildegarde, became an anchoress living in a cell attached to a church. In her teaching there are wonderful echoes of Hildegarde. She has a particular basic honesty, a tough tenacity to search out answers to her questions, and at the same time a remarkably comfortable friendly sweetness. She wrote down all her understanding but she talks straight to her reader as she must have talked to her friends and visitors, describing God who is 'unmade' and talking of the Trinity in homely, simple style because the things which she had seen, heard and felt were objective truth to her about which she wanted to talk freely.

Julian received strange and mysterious revelations, both in her body and in her mind. She balanced these revelations by thoughtful, contemplative understanding of them and developed an intuitive penetration into many of the perplexities of Christianity.

Her teaching is concerned with the all-embracingness of divine love, both received and given. In the light of this love, which to her was Ultimate Reality, every problem became unimportant and she saw all created things in a new dimension. She saw that the nature of the world and of the individual is as nothing compared to the infinity and timelessness of the God-ground; yet in another sense all is infinitely precious since it originates from and is sustained by that Reality itself. 'He is our clothing that, for love, wraps us up and winds us about; embraces us, all encloses us and hangs about us, for tender love; so that he can never leave us.'

Her whole theology rings with positive assurance – with joy and happiness in the unique fact that she and all beings are created at all. She sees in our very existence the amazing opportunity we are given to transcend the insignificant and to become that which is the whole meaning of our lives. To her such a 'that' was God the Father – for she was properly a woman of her century and thoroughly entrenched in the religious tradition and language of her age. Every creature who could begin to feel a new beingness was the Father's 'courteous' gift to his Son: 'For we are his bliss, we are his prize, we are his worship, we are his crown.'

She talks of God as easily as did Hildegarde:

> Some of us believe that he is all-mighty and *may* do all, and that he is all-wisdom and *can* do all. But that he is all-love and *will* do all, *there* we fall short.
>
> God is nearer to us than our own soul for he is the ground in whom our soul stands; and he is the means which keeps the substance and senses together, so that they shall never part. For our soul sits in God in very rest; and our soul stands in God in endless love. And therefore, if we want to have knowing of our soul, and communion and loving with it, we need to seek into our God in whom it is enclosed.
>
> *The Revelations of Divine Love of Julian of Norwich*

And, like Hildegarde, she knew no division between God and the world:

> Nature has been tested in the fire of tribulation, and in it was found no lack or defect. Thus are nature and grace of one accord. For grace is God, and unmade nature is God also. He is two in manner of working but one in love; and neither of these works without the other – they cannot be parted.

Julian *delighted* in God. And her delight took her to that miraculous land of awareness, to the new world within the known world, where all things show a translucent innerness.

> Truth sees God and wisdom beholds God, and of these two comes forth the third, and that is a holy marvelling delight in God, which is love.
>
> *Ibid*

Some of her words are quoted even today. In particular people draw comfort from one of her conversations with Jesus:

> Our good Lord answered all the questions and doubts that I might make, saying full and comfortably in this way: I will make all things well. I shall make all things well. I may make all things well, and I can make all things well; and so you shall see for yourself that all things shall be well.
>
> *Ibid*

Richard Rolle, a Yorkshire mystic of the same century, in a different way conveyed some of the same clear certainty:

> While I prayed to heaven with my whole heart, suddenly, I cannot tell in what manner, I felt in me the noise of song and received the most enchanting heavenly melody which stayed with me in my mind. And then my thought was changed to a constant song of mirth, and praises came into my meditation and into my prayers and psalm-saying. I gave out the same sound as I heard from then on, with a feeling of great inward sweetness. I burst out singing what before I had said, but only in private and alone before my Maker. Nothing was known by them that saw me, for if they had known it they would have honoured me too much and so I would have lost part of the most fair flower and should have felt forsaken.
>
> In the meantime wonder caught me that I should be taken up to so great a mirth while I was still solitary; and that God should give such gifts to me, ones that I knew not even what to ask for and that I could hardly believe that any man, even the holiest, could receive in this life. Therefore I believe that this is not given for any special reason, but freely to whom Christ will; nevertheless I also believe no man receives it unless he specially loves the name of Jesus, and honours it so much that he never lets it pass from his mind except in sleep.
>
> *The Fire of Love and the Mending of Life*

The other great English mystic was the unknown author of *The Cloud of Unknowing* – more profound than Richard Rolle and a great teacher:

For of all the other creatures and their works, yes, and of the works of God's self, may a man through grace have full head of knowing, and well he can think of them: but of God himself can no man think. And therefore I would leave all that thing which I can think, and choose to my love that thing that I cannot think. For why; He may well be loved but not thought. By love he may be gotten and holden; but by thought never. And therefore, although it be good sometimes to think of the kindness and the worthiness of God in special; and although it be a light and a part of contemplation: yet nevertheless in this work it shall be cast down and covered with a cloud of forgetting. And you shall step above it stalwartly but yearningly with a devout and a pleasing stirring of love, and try to pierce that darkness above you. And smite upon that thick cloud of unknowing with a sharp dart of longing love; and go not away from there for anything that befalls.

When I left these English mystics I felt that they had been the ones who had kept alive a particularly affectionate and happy side of the dark religion that was then Christianity, and that to find its continuation beyond the Middle Ages might be difficult. And indeed there was never again quite the same simple holiness. But down the centuries other voices spoke, sometimes movingly.

One was the sixteenth century St John of the Cross, that strange dark figure of Spanish mysticism, who entered the Carmelite life to find solitude and austerity and then was imprisoned for his reforms. For some months he was kept in barbarous conditions in a cell in Toledo but it was during this solitary incarceration that he experienced 'divine raptures' which led to his passionate books, *The Ascent of Mount Carmel* and *The Dark Night of the Soul*. That last title is a phrase kept alive in religious language ever since because it expresses the anguish many of us go through at some point on our journey. St John's teachings are not at all easy but some of his poems are unforgettable:

> My Beloved is the mountains,
> And lonely wooded valleys,
> Strange islands,
> And resounding rivers,
> The sighing of love-stirring breezes,

> The tranquil night
> At the time of rising dawn,
> Silent music,
> Sounding solitude,
> The supper that refreshes and deepens love.

In great contrast, the seventeenth century monk, Brother Lawrence, tells us that when he was eighteen he was a footman and 'a great awkward fellow, who broke everything'. But he had a sudden conversion which filled him with the love of God. He became a Carmelite lay-brother and expected to suffer for his faults; and indeed for four years he was very troubled in his mind. But then he passed on to 'a perfect liberty and continual joy' which he was able to carry into the kitchen where he had been set to work. He found that his meditation and his cooking became one and the same.

> And it was observed that in the greatest hurry of business in the kitchen he still preserved his recollection and heavenly-mindedness. He was never hasty nor loitering, but did each thing in its season, with an even tranquillity of spirit. 'The time of business,' said he, 'does not with me differ from the time of prayer; and in the noise and clutter of my kitchen, while several persons are at the same time calling for different things, I possess God in as great tranquillity as if I were upon my knees at the Blessed Sacrament.
>
> *The Practice of the Presence of God*

Again, Brother Lawrence seemed unrepeatable. But in the same century the words of Thomas Traherne also filled me with a sense of the mystery. He seems to say what each of us longs to experience:

> You never enjoy the world aright, till the sea itself flows in your veins, till you are clothed with the heavens, and crowned with the stars: and perceive yourself to be the sole heir of the whole world, and more so because men are in it who are every one sole heirs as well as you. Till you can sing and rejoice and delight in God, as misers do in gold, and kings in sceptres, you never enjoy the world . . .
>
> *Centuries of Meditation*

When I first read William Blake, the eighteenth century poet and painter, I found him tantalizingly obscure. His pictures shone with a wonderful glory but his words were often full of gloom and his allegories were baffling and beyond me. Yet everything he did was full of mightiness and vision and eventually I became closer to his thought and found he was indeed writing about the act of awakening, of becoming, aware of the sacred nature of existence:

> If the doors of perception were cleansed every thing would appear to man as it *is*, infinite.
> For man has closed himself up, till he sees all things through narrow chinks of his cavern.

He describes the moment of new consciousness when time itself seems to disappear and all that there is appears timeless and infinite:

> To see a World in a Grain of Sand
> And a Heaven in a Wild Flower,
> Hold Infinity in the palm of your hand
> And Eternity in an hour.

Blake saw existence as the descent of the spirit into matter. This has been a commonly held view throughout religious history. It can lead either to the despising of matter or to being illumined by it. In a way it is the basis of all religion and perhaps only Taoism and Zen have transformed that initial descent by a different view of it altogether.

Blake was illumined by matter but knew that not everyone was: 'The tree which moves some to tears of joy is in the eyes of others only a green thing which stands in the way.' (Letters of William Blake)

He looked on human life not as a succession of once-only phenomena but more in the way a Hindu would see it – as particular manifestations of an eternal Being. When we are awake, he said, we live in eternity; asleep, we exist in time.

'He who sees the infinite in all things, sees God. He who sees the Ratio [all we have already known] only, sees himself only.'

He was greatly moved by the 'soul', not only in humans but in everything. He regarded the body as the appearance of the soul and said that if we had eyes to see beyond the outward form we would perceive the eternal renewal of being, even in the grave.

'Man's perceptions are not bounded by organs of perception; he perceives more than sense (tho' ever so acute) can discover.'

He looked upon the Christianity of his day as a false religion. He saw that the body, which religion had separated from the soul and cast out, was in truth a vital aspect of the soul – and that the senses, which religion viewed with suspicion and mistrust (and still does) were 'the chief inlets of the soul in this age'.

He was deeply inspired by Jesus (and detested Christianity's teaching about him). To him, Jesus was 'God become as we are, that we may be as he is . . . For the desire of Man being Infinite, the possession is Infinite and himself Infinite.'

Blake was bluntly honest and unpretentious and I greatly appreciated his insights – but I never ceased to find him difficult. He was a mixture of shining gold and dark black and seemed in the end to represent the Western spiritual journey itself. I had found it enriching and deeply moving. But I felt it was as though, with the weight of formalized religion always hovering just above their path like a heavy cloud, the people who moved on it toiled hard. Up until the Middle Ages, there was sparkle and dance in their journey but after then it was hard going.

As the theologian Matthew Fox says:

> Western civilization has preferred love of death to love of life to the very extent that its religious traditions have preferred redemption to creation, sin to ecstasy, and individual introspection to cosmic awareness and appreciation. Religion has failed people in the West as often as it has been silent about pleasure or about the cosmic creation, about the ongoing power of the flowing energy of the Creator, about original blessing.
>
> *Original Blessing*

Gerard Manley Hopkins might have agreed with him. He was a nineteenth century priest-poet. He passionately adored the God-penetrated universe and can restore, in a single verse, that sense of being part of the Mystery.

> And the azurous hung hills are his world-wielding shoulder
> Majestic – as a stallion stalwart, very violet-sweet! –
> These things, these things, were here and but the beholder

Wanting; which two when they once meet,
the heart rears wings bold and bolder
And hurls for him, O half hurls earth for him off under his feet.

Hurrahing in Harvest

4

The Way of the Christ

THE SPIRITUAL JOURNEY in the West was, for many centuries, the way of Christianity. In my life, in all our lives, it has been even if unconsciously the sounding board of our values and thoughts.

For a long time in my adult life I felt no link at all with the Jesus of the New Testament. Even as a child, the cosmic sense of God was always far more present to me than the stories of the Galilean prophet.

But once, when I was about fourteen and going through adolescent storms and nightmares, I had a strange and exceptional dream about Jesus. It was the more unusual because I never consciously thought about him at all. He was in a small room and was surrounded by people and some animals. He was dressed in a white robe as in all the conventional pictures and a dove was perched close to him. I was on the fringe of the crowd and he never noticed me. But as I looked at him, I experienced a feeling I had never known before of transformation and great peace. That was all that happened. But I never forgot the dream.

Later in my life, when I read and wrote about the medieval mystics and found them conveying a Christianity which broke the narrow confines of any that I had come across, I realized that to ignore the religion of my own background might be to lose sight of a readily available source of wisdom. So for a time I 'took up' Christianity, regularly visited a nearby Anglican Benedictine monastery where there were beautiful services and often went to church. It did not work in the way that I had hoped for. I found considerable ignorance of my own sources of wisdom – the medieval mystics and eastern religions. Everyone was very nice to me and I had long talks with the abbot of the monastery. But at no time did I feel any nearer to Christianity.

Yet my Jesus dream still remained with me and I felt I still hadn't really come close in any way to the Christ, the founder of Christianity. Was he any more than an inspired prophet? I knew that the four Gospels were written by people who had never met him; that St Paul, the nearest in time, had not met him either but seemed to have taken Jesus as a figurehead on which to pin his own visions. That in the fourth century the Roman emperor Constantine had adopted Christianity as a state religion and pronounced Jesus a god and that after that Christianity had flourished. All this did not incline me to Christianity. But the mystery remained – who was he? What was the power that had shaped so many nations? I decided to try to find out.

First of all I discovered, quite to my surprise, that Christianity didn't really settle down in Europe for hundreds of years. In fact there seemed to be three forms of it around until at least the Middle Ages. The most usual form was the Catholic Church inherited from the Romans with its legal dictums and dogmas, its bishops and priests and large monasteries, and its rituals. Farther west was another more mystical Christianity, the Celtic Church, which produced many wandering hermits and saints. And the third was that of the ordinary people, who still believed in a number of the old Celtic and Saxon gods and goddesses and still made offerings at streams and wells – although the deity might have acquired the title of saint. They practised fertility rites in the old way and believed in green men, elves and fairies and many other entities, as well as the Christian family of Father, Mother and Son.

But again, none of this seemed to have much to do with Jesus himself and I began to realize that it would be hard to disentangle the man from all the stories and institutions built around him. So I started once more on the search for his actual life.

Here there was more confusion, for three of the four Gospels didn't always say the same thing even when telling the same story while the fourth, that of St John, is regarded by historians as a philosophical interpretation of what Jesus said, rather than his actual words.

Scholars have decided now that Mark's Gospel was the first to be written and that Matthew's and Luke's are both based on Mark's – improving his style, correcting what were believed to be his mistakes, and changing what might be thought offensive. For instance, when Jesus blessed the children who were brought to him, the blunt Mark reported that Jesus was angry with the disciples who had rebuked the parents for bringing the children – while in Matthew and Luke this is dropped out. Mark did not seem to mind showing Jesus as angry, but Matthew and Luke, writing some time later, did not like referring to violent feelings on the part of Jesus and also had a much more reverential attitude to the disciples.

Luke alone recounts the story of the virgin birth. Was it taken from other ancient Greek, Zoroastrian and Egyptian myths of a god born to a virgin? Such myths had been central to all the great mystery religions of the Near East. In his efforts to portray Jesus as a god, did Luke believe that he would be accepted more readily with such a birth legend attached to him? We will never know. But since much of his life is in any case largely unknown, I decided it would be best to concentrate on what his followers go by – his sayings and his miracles.

In his sayings he seemed to show a warmth and breadth of vision that was foreign to the Jews, his kindred; and it was also unlike the Essenes, the brotherhood of monastically pure and spiritual men amongst whom it is thought he spent most of his adult life. The Jews expected a Messiah to be an ideal man. He should be superior in every way, able to overcome all things with his strong personality, above all a great leader whom the Jewish people could revere and obey. Such a man was not expected to break the law of Moses and declare: 'The Sabbath was made for man, not man for the Sabbath; so the Son of Man is lord even of the Sabbath'; nor to eat with sinners and say, 'I came not to call the righteous, but sinners.'

As well, his conduct with women outraged both the Jews and the Essenes. Women in that society were beneath consideration, at the most second-class citizens, and association with them outside the immediate family was frowned on. If they were menstruating they were not allowed inside the temple – a custom which became current in Christianity for some centuries afterwards. And they could be divorced at any time and instantly, with no hope of compensation. Yet Jesus engaged in deep discussions with women, including prostitutes. He allowed a prostitute to touch him, massaging his feet and lavishing kisses on him. The Gospel writers themselves were horrified and the fact that the story went through the sieve of their censorship shows that it must have occurred.

Such happenings did not endear him to the Jews yet his own famous sayings, on which much of Christian spirituality is based, were not original to him but came from the rich lore of Jewish literature itself. The first commandment from the Sermon on the Mount, for instance, can be found almost word for word in Deuteronomy and is in fact the great 'Listen Israel' confession of faith which every Jew should repeat morning and evening. The second commandment, 'You shall love your neighbour as yourself', can be found in Leviticus. We can be certain that Jesus was learned and knowledgeable and it is unlikely that the thought ever occurred to him that he was teaching a path other than the path of the Jews. What he did do was to bring life to the old teachings in a new and exciting way and with a great authority – the authority of one who has experienced what he says. But it was not masterful enough to convince the Jews that he was the new Messiah – they merely thought him pretentious.

Then, too, such noble sayings as 'The Kingdom of Heaven is within you' and 'My Father is greater than I' were not at all foreign to the religious spirit of the time (although Christians have always thought them to be a new development). In Greek religion (which was to influence Christianity more than the Hebrew) such understanding was to be found in many statements; and under the Egyptian and also the Buddhist influence of those centuries, the essence of the Christian message had long been preached.

So I decided that to arrive at the real Jesus I must look at any other sayings which might have set him apart from the spiritual masters of his time. There were many such sayings, but until this century they were not known and so have not yet been accepted into orthodox church teaching. They are the statements found in a cave in Egypt and often called the Secret Sayings of Jesus.

In 1945 a large jar was dug up in Nag-Hamadi. Inside it were forty-nine Coptic (Egyptian Christian) Gnostic works, the total amounting to 700 pages. They had been written by groups of Gnostic Christian sects living between the first and second centuries AD. The Gnostic cult was one which severely troubled the Christians, for it happily synchronized the beliefs of unorthodox Jews, the Greeks and the Persians and, worst of all, was engaged not on a good and moral life founded on Jesus, but on *gnosis* – knowledge of the true nature of things. St Paul warned against Gnosticism in strong terms. Nevertheless many Gnostics were devout Christians and one of the documents found in the Nag jar turned out to be of the greatest importance. It was another gospel – the Gospel of Thomas.

This gospel is still thought of as heretical by church authorities. But we should remember that the four Gospels of the New Testament were themselves selected by church leaders many years after Jesus' death and that they chose them from out of a large number of similar gospels in circulation during the second century. Those that were not selected – because they did not accord with the church teaching of the time – were just as likely as the approved four to contain genuine sayings of Jesus.

So the Gospel of Thomas can claim to be an authentic gospel, written at the same time as the ones we know, but either rejected by the church or – more likely – kept secret by the Gnostic sect who owned it and who probably used it as the basis of their practice. It is full of profound and mystical sayings of Jesus and helps to explain why his teachings came to dominate the Mediterranean world. Many of the sayings

are familiar to us from the New Testament but they have
been given a Gnostic sea-change and transformed by a new
and moving language. When I read the Gospel of Thomas I
felt that I had at last found the Jesus of my dream.

For instance, Jesus said:

> If they say to you, Whence have you come?
> say to them, We come from the light,
> the place where the light came into existence
> through itself alone . . .
> If they say to you, Who are you?
> say, We are his sons, and we are
> the elect of the living Father.
> If they ask you, What is the sign of your
> Father who is within you
> say to them, It is a movement and a rest.

'Light' has always been connected with clarity, transparency,
enlightenment. 'The place where the light came into existence'
is perhaps what the great mystic, Eckhart, calls 'the spark in
the soul, which neither time nor space touches'. Jesus might
also have been influenced by the belief, current at the time,
that people shared in the stuff of the cosmos, that light must
be seen with light, that the human eye was similar to God's
eyes, that only starlike eyes could contemplate the stars and
sunlike eyes the sun.

'Through itself alone' seemed to be about the Mystery,
that which transcends all we know, the Source and the
Origin. I came to think of it as a meditation phrase, one
which one keeps in the mind and gradually its meaning
becomes apparent. I found that particular phrase, almost
more than any other, evocative of the true journey towards
the unconditioned wonder.

And that amazing statement that the sign of the Father
within is 'a movement and a rest' reflected for me the Taoist
'letting go'; the end of action induced by desires and
attachment ('The way to use life is to do nothing through
acting. The way to use life is to do everything through
being.').

The disciples asked Jesus questions:

> On what day will the rest of the dead take place?
> And on what day does the new world come?

He said to them:
That rest for which you are waiting has come;
but you do not recognize it.

Gospel of Thomas

So the 'rest' was to be experienced then and there – it had come. What a mysterious statement! Life is rest when self-seeking stops, the self is forgotten and all existence affirms one's being. But the disciples had not recognized it. This must have been the Master pointing out the wonder of existence which the pupil has not yet opened his eyes to. In a similar saying, the disciples asked Jesus:

'When will the Kingdom come?'

He answered, 'It will not come by expectation: they will not say "see here" or "see there". But the Kingdom of the Father is spread upon the earth and men do not see it.'

The disciples had expectations of the imminent arrival of a 'Kingdom' that would transform the earth. But expectations built on such concepts are not based on reality and usually lead to disappointment – 'I went, but it was not what I had thought it would be.' If the disciples would stop looking for the invisible ('it will not come by expectation') and instead open their eyes to that which was spread before them, they would see the wonder of the Kingdom within all creation.

And Jesus said:
I am the light
which is over everything.
I am the All;
from me the All has gone forth,
and to me the All has returned.
Split wood: I am there.
Lift up the stone, and you will find me there.

Ibid

Jesus must have fully realized the light, or enlightenment, and now was enlightened. The cycle of going forth and returning to the inner reality was completed for Jesus. As the completed All, as Enlightenment itself, Jesus was present everywhere – in wood and under stones. When you are enlightened, the Buddha said, then the whole world is enlightened. In the Gnostic Gospel of Eve, Jesus said: 'In all things I am scattered, and from wherever you wish you collect me.'

And he said: 'Let him who seeks, not cease from seeking until he finds, and when he finds, he will be troubled, and when he has been troubled, he will marvel and he will reign over the All.'

Here is a powerful and evocative map of the journey for each of us. So often the journey includes a time of doubt, stress and confusion, or 'trouble'. But if it does not include wonder and 'marvel' it has barely begun.

He said:

> If those who lead you say to you: 'See, the Kingdom is in heaven,' then the birds of the heaven will precede you. If they say to you: 'It is is in the sea,' then the fish will precede you. But the Kingdom is within you and is without you. If you will know yourselves, then you will be known and you will know that you are the sons of the living Father. But if you do not know yourselves, then you are in poverty and you are poverty.
>
> *Gospel of Thomas*

Here is the sort of teaching rarely found in churches. If you think the Kingdom is in heaven and not here and now, then this concept of a place in the sky is more appropriate to birds – they'll get there first. The same with the sea and fishes. Here is the Kingdom now, he says, of which you are a part, so that it is both within and all around you. If you begin to know your true self (that which transcends the ego), then you will find the Kingdom and you will know and be known – because the knower and the known will be one. But if you never undertake this, your life will be poverty itself.

All the great religious teachers have stressed the importance of finding a ground which is deeper than the emotions and a sense of timelessness which transcends the intellect. Without such a reaching down and reaching up, the horizontal level of existence swamps us, we are carried away by the superficial power we give to objects and are swayed this way and that by every opinion we hear. The need for enlightenment, for actual *knowing*, is essential to being alive, and without it we are asleep or dead. Jesus pointed out this need in no uncertain terms and if he had taught for longer would, perhaps, have developed ways of spiritual practice which the ordinary person could follow, as did the Buddha. As it was, we can be quite sure that sayings such as these carried great spiritual authority, sufficient to account for his reputation in a land of teachers.

And indeed, the Gnostic sect to whom this gospel belonged may well have used his statements as the source of spiritual exercises – as themes for contemplation, or as koans. Such sayings are so profound that hermits, such as the Desert Fathers of the fourth century, would undoubtedly have committed their lives to the study of them.

I was very happy that I had found the Jesus I was looking for – the one who embodied enlightenment and who saw the sacred in all things. But this Jesus seemed unknown to Christianity itself and so a door that might have opened remained closed for me. But I still wanted to study the miracles.

It puzzled me then and still puzzles me that the majority of Christians value Jesus not for his wisdom but for his miracles. For instance, in a television interview, a bishop stated that if the bones of Jesus were ever discovered (which would imply that he had not been resurrected bodily) Christianity would be 'killed stone dead' and he himself would no longer remain in the Church.

This seems to place an enormous burden on an event which is historically vague, even if very vivid as a story. Did Jesus die on the cross? Was he resurrected bodily?

The second century St Irenaeus, I discovered, declared that Jesus had lived to an old age. He expresses great indignation against the 'false opinion' that would rob Jesus 'of that age which is both more necessary and more honourable than any other; that more advanced age, I mean, during which also as a teacher He excelled all others.' The historian Geoffrey Higgins, having noted that there was a big question mark about the crucifixion among second century Christians, says that the evidence of Irenaeus cannot be doubted and that it was good fortune which kept the document he wrote out of the hands of those who would have destroyed it in order to make the Christ story consistent.

In fact there is no account of Jesus actually leaving the tomb and his appearance was not generally visible to everybody but only to certain believers – and even they had to have their faith awakened before they could recognize him. Mary Magdalen thought he was a gardener and the two men walking to Emmaus did not recognize their companion until their eyes were opened. Historians now think that the earliest believers did indeed claim to have seen Jesus in visions and that the later evangelists dramatized the visions and made them into objective facts. The latest scholarship, which seems to accord more with Irenaeus, has dated the birth of Jesus to 12 BC, which means that he lived until he was in his mid-forties at least.

I wondered about the miracles he accomplished while he was alive. I had never seen them as important, even as an impressionable child, but most people did and if they were a reflection of his teaching then perhaps they were right. I looked around for explanations and found one which seemed both reasonable and recent. It came from Ian Wilson, a Roman Catholic, who suggested that the miracles were based on hypnotism. Was hypnotism a way for Jesus to teach? By curing the sick did he bring them closer to his message?

Hypnotism is certainly a well-established way of healing. Wilson quotes the case of the hypnotist, Peter Casson, well known for his medical work, who was asked to cure a woman unable for fifteen years to close her hand or grip with it after a car accident. All operations had been unsuccessful but after only one hypnosis session with Casson her hand was back to normal. 'Effectively her "cure" was achieved by commands little different from those which Jesus was said to have used in curing the paralytic by Jerusalem's Sheep Pool,' says Wilson in his book, *Jesus: The Evidence*.

He points out that hypnosis was certainly practised in the mystery religions of the time. And the power that Jesus used must have been both famous and yet not considered divine because he sent out his disciples to do the same work of curing disease, and also gave them 'authority over unclean spirits'. Exorcism, like hypnotism, was one of the practices of the Jewish Hasidim sect.

Jesus undoubtedly possessed a great authority in this field (although unable to succeed in the place where he had grown up and where everyone knew him!). Although he was not unique in his powers (there were other famous hypnotists or 'miracle-workers' of the day, such as Hanina ben Dosa who was also, like Jesus, credited with curing a sick child) yet his successes were so many that his miracles seemed to become the chief basis for his popularity.

Wilson believes that two deeply held convictions sustained him in this work. One was that God was speaking and working through him and the other that the end of the world was close.

Quite apart from the healing but perhaps connected with hypnosis, there is also the probability that there was a mystery religion connected with his powers – which the New Testament would not reveal because it would be confined to initiates. When Jesus himself was undergoing a form of initiation – baptism by John – he saw a bird. It was, he said, 'the Spirit of God', a dove, which he knew to be a vision. As we know, the flight of a bird has always been identified with the journeys of the shaman, and this tradition was still very much alive at that time. The historian, Dr. Morton Smith, points out that:

> The vision of a bird also occurs in early mystery religion initiations as in one Greek magical papyrus description in which an initiate, after lying naked in a sheet and repeating a prescribed chant, is told to expect to see 'a sea-hawk flying down' as a sign that unity with the deity had been achieved. Such initiations were commonly followed by a period of self-enforced privation, reminiscent of Jesus's forty days in the wilderness.
>
> *Clement of Alexandria and a Secret Gospel of Mark*

The nakedness of the initiate is another link pointing to a mystery cult. It is thought that Jesus was naked when baptized by John and there are several references to his belief in nakedness as part of what was perhaps an initiation ceremony. There is the mysterious incident of the young man in the Garden of Gethsemane who wore 'a linen cloth cast about his naked body' and who 'fled from them naked' when the disciples caught hold of him. Wilson asks, 'Was this one of the occasions on which Jesus took a favoured disciple, through hypnosis, on a journey to the Kingdom of God?' (*Jesus: The Evidence*)

Then there is a passage in the Gospel of Thomas, when the disciples asked Jesus when they would see him. He answered:

> When you undress yourselves and are not ashamed,
> and take your clothing
> and lay them under your feet
> like little children
> and tread on them;
> then you will become sons of the Living One
> and you will have no fear.

A letter pointing to a mystery cult was written by an early Church Father, Clement of Alexandria, who lived at the end of the second century. He speaks of a secret Gospel of Mark which contained instructions for 'special' followers of Jesus. They were referred to as 'those who were being perfected' or 'those who are being initiated into the great mysteries'.

Part of the mystery concerned resurrection, or raising from the dead. A rich young man is referred to as dying and being buried.

> And going near, Jesus rolled away the stone from the door to the tomb. And straightway, going in where the youth was, he stretched forth his hand and raised him, seizing his hand. But the youth, looking upon him, loved him and began to beseech him that he might be with him. And going out of the tomb they came into the house of the youth, for he was rich. And after six days Jesus told him what to do and in the evening the youth came to him, wearing a linen cloth over his naked body. And he remained with him that night, for Jesus taught him the mystery of the Kingdom of God. And thence, arising, he returned to the other side of the Jordan.
>
> *Clement of Alexandria and a Secret Gospel of Mark*

Clement assures Theodore, the recipient of the letter – who had obviously heard strange rumours of the incident – that there was nothing in Mark's 'secret' gospel to justify the belief that Jesus and the young man were both naked together for the initiation.

In fact, Christians need not feel too uncomfortable about such nakedness. The Greeks and Romans saw nothing shameful in the naked body. And removing the clothes was likely to have been the secret ritualistic outer gesture for a spiritual uncovering. In the Gospel of Thomas, Jesus makes a number of references to such an uncovering as it could be conceived in the highest spiritual sense:

> Do not speak falsely
> and what you hate, do not do.
> For all things are revealed before heaven.
> For there is nothing hidden which shall not be manifested,
> and there is nothing which is covered which will remain
> without being uncovered.

Jesus as a person came alive to me through the Gospel of Thomas in a way that he had never done by reading the official Gospels. He seemed such an unusual Jew. He was open and unconventional, never afraid to challenge the letter of the law when he thought it was destroying the spirit. He befriended and helped women (even giving help to a woman on the Sabbath) and did the same for outcasts, the poor, the mad and the sick. Above all, he was one who felt the luminous presence of Abba, 'the Father', directing his actions, and it was to Abba that he committed himself wholly. He hoped to share his enlightened state with others and he gave a teaching which brought him renown.

His charisma was so great that he had to escape the crowds and sought solitude often. In his relaxed moments he preferred the company of wine-bibbers and prostitutes to that of the respectable.

> No one revelled in life more than Jesus. He scandalized his contemporaries who labelled him a glutton and a wine-bibber. When the drink ran out, Jesus made an even better brew, enough to drown the whole village according to John's account. Affirmation that life is for living, and compassion to enable it to be lived were his hallmarks.
>
> Ian Wilson, *Jesus: the Evidence*

So that was the person of Jesus – a good deal more attractive to me than the usual conventional portait. Yet I felt that there was still a great mystery about him which evaded both the sociable, welcoming Jesus and the secret initiator into a hidden cult. The Jesus of the Gospel of Thomas seemed to be nearest the mystery and it remains one of my most-read books.

Others too have felt the mystery and down the centuries he has inspired some of the greatest literature, music and art the world has known. In it he is regarded less as Jesus the man and more as the Christ, the Way. Many Catholic Christians believe, for instance, that in some way unfathomable to humanity the person of Jesus Christ contains the whole explanation of existence – not so much in his historical concreteness but as the 'cosmic Christ', a spirit of the universe.

The scientist-priest, Teilhard de Chardin, says:

> Once we make up our minds to take the words of Revelation literally – and to do so is the idea of all true religion – then the whole mass of the Universe is gradually bathed in light. And just as science shows us, at the lower limits of matter, an ethereal fluid in which everything is immersed and from which everything emerges, so at the upper limits of Spirit a mystical ambience appears in which everything floats and everything converges.
>
> *Let Me Explain*

The cosmic sense of Christ is finely expressed in Teilhard's ideas. He goes on to say:

> What is the supreme and complex reality for which the divine operation moulds us? It is revealed to us by St Paul and St John. It is the quantitative repletion and the qualitative consummation of all things: it is the mysterious Pleroma, in which the substantial *one* and the created *many* fuse without confusion in a *whole* which, without adding anything essential to God, will nevertheless be a sort of triumph and generalization of being . . .
>
> What is the active centre, the living link, the organizing soul of the Pleroma? St Paul again, proclaims it with his resounding voice: it is he in whom everything is reunited, and in whom all things are consummated – through whom the whole created edifice receives its consistence – Christ dead and risen . . .
>
> We shall now see with a wave of joy that the divine omnipresence translates itself within our universe by the network of organizing forces of the total Christ. God exerts pressure, in us and upon us – through the intermediary of all the powers of heaven, earth and hell – only in the act of forming and consummating Christ who saves and sur-- animates the world. And since, in the course of this operation,

Christ himself does not act as a dead or passive point of convergence, but as a centre of radiation for the energies which lead the universe back to God through his humanity, the layers of divine action finally come to us impregnated with his organic energies.

The Divine Milieu

For Teilhard and for many deeply reflecting Christians, God is the Ultimate Being who is expressed in the perfect man, Jesus Christ. So for Teilhard and all those others the whole of evolution is prearrangedly heading towards the Pleroma, a point in time when conscious, supremely personal humankind will be united and one with Christ the Omega-point, the heart of the universe.

This is a noble concept but I felt, once more, that the mystery of Christ was still eluding even that capturing. I felt I must continue my journey, very much the richer for the Gospel of Thomas but not, finally, settling down into belief in God the Father and Christ the Son, however universalized that Christ was shown to be. But one of Teilhard's prayers has stayed with me ever since:

O God, whose call precedes the first of our movements, grant me the desire to desire being – that by means of that divine thirst which is your gift, the access to the great waters may open wide within me. Do not deprive me of the sacred taste for being, that primordial energy, that very first point of our points of rest .... And you whose loving wisdom forms me out of all the forces and all the hazards of the earth . . . grant that, after having desired, I may believe, and believe ardently and above all things, in your active presence.

Ibid

5

The Eastern Journey

BOTH THE CELTS and the Hindus came originally from the same people – a vigorous, inspired prehistoric race known as the Battle-Axe People, whose mark was a perforated stone battle-axe and whose home was in what is now southern Russia. The ancestors of the Celts journeyed to Europe and Scandinavia; a different migration spread into India. The languages spoken by the Celts come from the same source as Sanskrit, the classical language of the Hindus. And the Celtic languages themselves have always been called Indo-European, acknowledging our cousinly relationship to India.

When I discovered this, I looked immediately to India to see how the spirit had expressed itself there. I found a great deal that was a revelation to me and of immense value – a wisdom that seemed far deeper than anything in the West. But of the Celtic sense of the numinous there was none.

If I had not turned to the East, though, I would have missed a cosmic dimension, one that I believe is essential for growth. All that I had sensed and half understood could be put into a far wider religious framework than any I had come across in the West. For at the heart of eastern spirituality is the belief in the 'self', the knowledge of one's own true being; the understanding that one's own consciousness is God. Everything that exists is an aspect of the One Reality – for which the word God seems a pale shadow. 'O Thou, before whom all words recoil' says Shankara, and that 'Thou' is the unity in which the world lives and moves. When, through ignorance or blindness, the unity is lost sight of, then the world appears to be comprised of a vast multitude of separate beings and things, including ourselves. But when the unity is seen as the Whole, transcending all its innumerable parts, although not separate from them, as a person transcends his limbs yet is them all, the unity is then the perfect nature of all that exists.

To the Hindu, the awareness of God as the undifferentiated Ground gives a feeling of true identity, of having come home to the real self at last. Hence God is often spoken of as the 'self', the realization of one's own sacred beingness.

From its earliest days – at least 4000 years ago, according to historians – Indian religion has practised yoga (the practices for training the mind and the heart as well as the body). And from the beginning to the present day there have been the sages, those teachers of spiritual paths who often spent long periods away from humanity in solitude in the forests.

I became particularly attached to one such sage, Ramana Maharshi, who founded an ashram in Tiruvannamalai and who died in 1950.

Ramana seemed somehow to teach the essence of all that I found valuable in Hinduism. He taught the two basic ways of seeing into the nature of things – the first by asking the question 'Who am I?', and the second by surrender to the self.

The first – self-enquiry – was directed towards consciousness itself. He believed that we misunderstand our true nature when we identify ourselves with the feelings and sensations of the body. Because we think of the body as the self, we believe that the world is composed of a multiplicity of other bodies all containing separate selves. We dwell only on outward appearances and are misled by them. A universe of names and forms dominates our thinking. But consciousness itself is beyond name and form, it is the self, and the way for each one of us to experience this consciousness is to give up identifying with the objects of consciousness.

So it is the sense of 'I' that is the self in Ramana's teaching. 'He proclaimed the Absolute as the Self, the "I am" in each individual life, ever being itself.' When I thought about this I realized that there were many occasions when the real sense of 'I' was missing in me. For instance, I could be too conscious of other people, more conscious of them than I was of myself. I could be dominated by my desire to agree, to please, and then my own sense of 'I' was obscured. My confidence in myself and my own opinion was often lacking and I was easily swayed by more self-assured voices. And too often things 'happened' to me and I did not seem able to be in control of my own life.

A clear sense of 'I', even in quite small ways, seemed to me the right step. If I could live in 'I' rather than moving out of it all the time, I knew I would feel stronger. When a king is on his throne, runs a Tibetan saying, his courtiers come to him; but if he gets off his throne and follows any of them, he loses it. I was constantly losing the throne and knew that I needed to stay there.

Ramana's method of self-enquiry was to keep the question 'Who am I' continually in one's mind. After doing this for some time I did indeed come to feel that many of the things I had thought important were irrelevant – that the 'I' that is so often identified with events was of a different and lesser order than a more true 'I'.

Ramana believed that all the thoughts and feelings of the ego, the small self, would cease their domination automatically when the 'I' was fully realized:

Everyone is the Self and, indeed, is infinite. Yet each person mistakes his body for his Self . . . Consciousness is the Self of which everyone is aware. No one is ever away from his Self and therefore everyone is in fact Self-realized; only – and this is the great mystery – people do not know this and want to realize the Self. Realization consists only in getting rid of the false idea that one is not realized. It is not anything new to be acquired . . . Once the false notion 'I am the body' or 'I am not realized' has been removed, Supreme Consciousness or the Self alone remains and in people's present state of knowledge they call this 'Realization'.

To those who have not realized the Self as well as to those who have, the world is real. But to the former, Truth is adapted to the form of the world, whereas to the latter Truth shines as the formless Perfection and the Substratum of the world.

The Teachings of Ramana Maharshi

Keeping that 'Who am I' query in my mind certainly helped me to become more myself. But in so doing, it raised the question of individuality and here I felt that neither Ramana nor Hinduism generally took this into account. It seemed that it was swept away with the 'falsity' of ego and I felt it wasn't like that. What I was experiencing was a stronger sense of being a proper human and it felt right. To be a true individual, able to make use of all the good qualities of human beingness was surely what one was here on this earth for? I felt that Ramana was too dismissive of the joy and delight of simply being a person. Odd things I remembered came back to me. 'God is an angel in an angel, and a stone in a stone, and a straw in a straw,' said John Donne. And a human in a human surely? I did realize that it was a question of identification and that if one identified solely with humanity one was in trouble. But obstinately I still felt that there was nothing intrinsically false about being human.

I was puzzled. What Ramana was saying was right and yet it seemed to miss personhood out. He said:

> 'I exist' is the only permanent, self-evident experience of every one. Nothing else is so self-evident as 'I am'. What people call 'self-evident' viz. the experience they get through the senses, is far from self-evident. The Self alone is That. So, to do Self-analysis and be 'I am' is the only thing to do. 'I am' is reality. I am *this* or *that* is unreal.'

> *Ibid*

And yet being the this or that of a human seemed more and more real to me and I found myself at one with the questioner who asked Ramana how to realize the self.

'The I-thought,' he replied, 'is the root thought. If the root is pulled out, all the rest is at the same time uprooted. Therefore seek the root "I"; question yourself: "Who am I?"; find out the source of the "I". Then the problem will vanish and the pure Self alone will remain.'

Persistently, the questioner asked: 'But how am I to do it?'

Ramana answered: 'The "I" is always there, whether in deep sleep, in dream, or in the waking state. The one who sleeps is the same as the one who is now speaking. There is always the feeling of "I". If it were not so you would have to

deny your existence. But you do not. You say "I am". Find
out who is.'

Thoroughly muddled, the questioner nevertheless kept at
it:

'I still do not understand. You say the "I" is now the false
"I". How am I to eliminate the wrong "I"?'

Ramana replied: 'You need not eliminate any false "I".
How can "I" eliminate itself? All that you need do is to find
out its origin and stay there. Your effort can extend only so
far. Then the Beyond will take care of itself. You are helpless
there. No effort can reach it.'

I decided I would follow this excellent advice and stay
where I was, feeling my 'I' to be expressed in my humanity
and waiting for the Beyond to take me further towards the
origin of 'I'.

And here Ramana's second teaching on self-surrender was
illuminating. In this he used the term 'God' although for him
it was never the over-simple external God of many westerners.
Self-surrender meant surrendering the ego to God by way of
realizing one's own limitations and helplessness, and by
substituting God's will for one's own; by accepting all that is
to be done without ever claiming any action as one's own,
thus removing all sense of 'me' and 'mine'. Surrender in this
way does not involve the intellect so much as the will, for it is
a continual giving up of identity; a giving away of the feeling
of oneself as the 'doer' of one's actions.

Ramana says:

> Surrender once and for all and be done with desires. So long as
> the sense of being the doer remains desire does also. Therefore
> the ego remains. But once this goes the Self shines forth in its
> purity. The sense of being the doer is the bondage, not the
> actions themselves. 'Be still and know that I am God.' Here
> stillness is total surrender without a vestige of individuality.
> Stillness will prevail and there will be no agitation of the mind.
> Agitation of mind is the cause of desire, of the sense of being
> the doer, of personality. If that is stopped, there is quiet . . .
> Would you bear your load on your head when you are
> travelling in a train? It carries you and your load whether the
> load is on your head or on the floor of the train. You are not
> lessening the burden of the train by keeping it on your head

but only straining yourself unnecessarily. Similar is the sense of doership in the world by individuals.

Ibid

And from Thomas Merton's introduction to the *Bhagavad Gita*:

> To live with the true consciousness of life centred in Another is to lose one's self-important seriousness and thus to live life as 'play' in union with a Cosmic Player. It is He alone that one takes seriously. But to take Him seriously is to find joy and spontaneity in everything for everything is gift and grace. In other words to live selfishly is to bear life as an intolerable burden. To live selflessly is to live in joy, realizing by experience that life itself is love and gift. To be a lover and a giver is to be a channel through which the Supreme Giver manifests His love in the world.

I knew from the folly of my own past actions that it is arrogant to believe that one always knows best for oneself. It is a narrow and visionless way of looking to believe that one can always 'act' without reference to what Taoists term the 'Way' of things. I had long been aware that when I allowed myself to wait and listen instead of springing into action, the results were usually much better. But it did need the effort of trust. The trust lay in believing that life is intrinsically good and right, and that what is provided for one right now is the proper and appropriate condition for this moment. I saw too that to attempt to manipulate present existence for one's own benefit is to impose a stultifying and deadening concept onto a living reality.

It seemed to me that there was a way of being, one that I called 'deep life', in which, like a dog who eats grass when he feels sick, one is empowered to know what to do by itself; that this way of being does demand a surrender of self-will; but that having made this surrender there is a feeling of miraculous release. I came to feel that Ramana's advice to drop the 'doer' was a way of dropping a heavy and unnecessary burden. It was as though the sea rises and falls and the wind blows but not because of me; in the same way the steps are taken, the food is eaten, the book is read, but there is no self involved.

When I left Ramana (and 'leaving' did not imply giving up,

but more a change of outlook) I turned to mainstream Buddhism. Here I found much the same advice. 'In the walking just the walking, in the sitting just the sitting, in the thinking just the thought,' said the Buddha. He did not leave room for what to him was the imaginary self. For he, like Ramana, taught that the main cause of suffering is the belief in a separate ego. In truth, there is no such thing as a self, he said, there is only the endless flux of sensations and thoughts and feelings that we take for reality and believe to be self-powered. The flow of endless appearances that make up the 'world' are all proceeding from each other in a minutely determined chain of cause and effect. But there is also that which transcends the chain; and enlightenment is the experience of finding that unconditioned and timeless dimension.

At the time that I became interested in Buddhism (where I stayed for many years) a good teacher had arrived in London from Thailand. His name was Dhiravamsa and he helped clear up some points for me:

> Feelings are very important if we are to bring about clear understanding of truth. Whenever there is contact there arises a feeling, and we have contact with things all the time. Even when we sit silent quietly in the room we have contact with something and then feeling must arise. Now if we say 'I am this', or 'this is mine', or 'this is my feeling', then how can we be permanently happy? It is not possible because if something you grasp (which you think belongs to you) goes wrong, you feel unhappy. This can be seen in daily life very easily. But, if you are free from the 'I', what is there to suffer? Who can suffer? Suffering will be unable to arise and at the same time there is nobody to suffer.
>
> *The Way of Non-Attachment*

Dhiravamsa advised the practice of paying attention as an important way to selfless awareness, and this exercise is one I have continued to find endlessly useful – in fact I now believe it is the essential spiritual practice. On the subject of Vipassana meditation, he said:

> The whole spirit of it lies in full attention or complete attention. This is very important. If we actually attend to what we do, what we see, what we come across, what we

experience, then there is no waste of energy, no waste of time for seeing the truth, the living movement of life . . . The natural process of paying attention is to let things flow, not to exclude yourself or anything else and then the whole process of attention is an inclusive process, which is the dynamic process of living. Some people may call this a kind of movement in silence, or movement in the unknown. The unknown is that which cannot be given a name, a concept . . . so meditation in your daily life is to be very attentive to everything. Then you can feel lively with your life, with your experiences without being attached. You will become realistic, looking at life, seeing it for what it is. You will learn to accept whatever arises and to practise acceptance in action, not the idea. Beliefs, doubts and uncertainties are replaced by understanding and seeing.

Ibid

The Vipassana meditation exercise that Dhiravamsa talked of was one that I came to adopt and still use. It is expecially useful when my mind becomes obsessed with something – some trouble or preoccupation. Then I firmly remove myself from the scene by practising the meditation which, for me, consists in using the words 'this is' or 'there is' rather than 'I am'. At such times I use it in every situation. For instance, 'There is a scrubbing of potatoes'; 'this is a head of hair to be brushed'; 'at this moment there is a reading of a book' – even 'there is a tooth being drilled by the dentist'. It has the effect of instant release from self-preoccupation and remains for me a very valued exercise.

Another thing that Dhiravamsa said impressed me deeply:

The second factor of Vipassana is awareness itself. The Buddha gave advice to an old man who came to ask him about the practice. He was getting old and he wondered about a short cut. People always want to find a short cut. The Buddha said, 'Have awareness constantly and look at the world as emptiness.'

Ibid

I felt that to have awareness constantly was something comprehensible I could aim to do. Awareness was wide attention writ large. But to see the world as emptiness – that phrase rang bells deep inside me. I knew what it was like when the world seemed exceptionally solid and overwhelming – that always happened when I was very involved emotionally. But at other times, and increasingly often since I came to know the eastern religions, I had felt the lightness of the world – sometimes almost as a transparency, as though objects could float about and it would not surprise me. It always made me smile, this secret lightness of things, for I knew it would seem quite mad to most people.

It was a happy state and in order to evoke it I invented a formula to say. If I said to myself: 'Here (meaning within myself) is Reality, and there (meaning everything outside) is appearance', I could bring about the state at once. When things are seen as appearances they are no longer solid and in fact they seem both empty and yet at the same time full of their own elusive enchantment.

I felt this might be a step towards what the Buddha talked of in that phrase 'to see the world as emptiness'. For me, that sort of saying seemed more valuable than the emphasis on morality and ethics which seemed to dominate a lot of mainstream Buddhism, although that too had its own place.

All in all, I rejoiced in the eastern spiritual journey which had given me quite a lot of valuable work and taken me several years. The wisdom of the Hindus and Buddhists had enriched my understanding immeasurably.

But I was by no means finished with the East, for it was when I journeyed (metaphorically) to China and encountered Taoism that I at once felt truly at home. Throughout the other religions, particularly Buddhism, the emphasis had mostly been concerned with understanding and consequently mastering the self. But there had been little about the Mystery and nothing about delight in it. But the very first poem in Lao Tzu's *Tao Te Ching* took me at once to the heart of the Mystery.

> Existence is beyond the power of words
> To define:
> Terms may be used
> But are none of them absolute.
> In the beginning of heaven and earth there were no words,
> Words came out of the womb of matter;
> And whether a man dispassionately

Sees to the core of life
Or passionately
Sees the surface,
The core and the surface are essentially the same,
Words making them seem different
Only to express appearance.
If name be needed, wonder names them both:
From wonder into wonder
Existence opens.

It seemed to me that 'dispassionately seeing to the core of life' had been the basis of Buddhism, and of Ramana's teaching too. But 'passionately seeing the surface' was the other way never talked about in those religions. It was the old Celtic way and I believed it truly led 'from wonder into wonder'.

I found that Chinese thought was full of reverence for the living world. It was expressed in their paintings where tree and mountain, man and space blended into one. This is the principle of *li* (innermost reality, or 'suchness') – that which transcends form and yet is inherent in every atom. For example, if you are a painter you should identify yourself with the *li* of what you are painting so that the painting reveals the essential nature of itself. However carefully and faithfully the picture may reflect external shapes and colours if it is not based on that intuitive apprehension of *li* it will not be worthy of the art.

Hence the great landscape paintings accentuated sharp mountain peaks which seemed to float in space – and yet every leaf was evident in the tree dominating the foreground. Such was the make-up of Taoism, the infinite and the immediate merged into one.

Existence – the Way – the nameless – yes, here I felt at home. Here there was no need to sort out what was a false self and what was a true; no need to examine the nature of consciousness. Here all that was needed was to experience true wonder at the very fact of existence.

The Taoist 'Way' resembled my own feeling of 'deep life' and the Taoist advice was to let go of fixed ideas and self-imposed boundaries and see what life really is (in a way, what Dhiravamsa was teaching, too). But here it was not words but movement. To flow into it and with it. Accept what comes along with a joyful awareness. To see the universe as the creative dance of the Tao and move in step with it. The realm of Tao is the realm of inner essence, of reality. To live in accord with the Tao is to live at one with one's being. The Tao is both the Way and the Goal.

> The surest test if a man be sane
> Is if he accepts life whole, as it is,
> Without needing by measure or touch to understand
> The measureless untouchable source
> Of its images,
> The measureless untouchable source
> Of its substances,
> The source which, while it appears dark emptiness,
> Brims with a quick force
> Farthest away
> And yet nearest at hand
> From oldest times unto this day,
> Charging its images with origin:
> What more need I know of the origin
> Than this?
>
> Lao Tzu, *Tao Te Ching*

But, much though I loved the Tao, Taoism itself was no longer a living religion. Its spirit, though, had flowed into Chinese Buddhism. Buddhism had migrated to China in the early centuries AD and had made a big impact. Over two or three hundred years it blended with Taoism to form Ch'an, a term meaning awareness meditation. Ch'an eventually became Zen in Japanese and thus Zen became the next step on my journey.

6

The Chinese Journey

BEFORE TURNING TO Japanese Zen, though, I stayed with China a bit longer and in fact have come back to it over and over again in my spiritual journey and probably always will. In China's early days, it seemed so much the land of spirituality, subtlety and also robust good humour. In the days of the Ch'an masters the teaching they gave was direct and individual. They dispensed with theology but did believe that the 'ten thousand things' – existence itself – was sacred. They said that what we experience through our senses is Ultimate Reality but we rarely experience it in that way because we do not allow the space and silence for it to be itself.

'Our original nature is, in highest truth, void, silent, pure; it is glorious and mysterious peaceful joy – and that is all. Enter deeply into it by awakening to it yourself. That which is before you is it, in all its fullness, utterly complete,' said Huang Po in the ninth century.

This, to me, was the easiest and most effective theology of all.

I found that one of the original Ch'an teachings is condensed into a form known as the Ox-herding pictures, a series of ten paintings which tell a story. When I visited Korea (at one time a Buddhist country), I discovered the pictures were painted on the outside of the main temple in Seoul and that it was possible to move round the temple and take the same journey as the boy takes when he searches for and finds his lost ox.

I too am on that journey – as we all are – and so I have related it here.

The first picture shows a boy searching for his ox. The ox must have been the most commonly used animal in China, as it once was in Europe, and so he lost something really vital when it disappeared. In these pictures the ox is meant to represent our original nature, that which we lose sight of when we take the world at a horizontal level only and allow it no heights or depths; when we become identified with the things of the world to such an extent that we can't see our own original identity. In fact the ox has never really gone astray, we have never really lost our original sacred nature, but we no longer have knowledge of it, it is crowded out by our deluded desires.

So the boy is at the stage when the life he is living is too real for him. We can all recognize ourselves in that situation. When we start our adult life we believe the world to be just as we see it, without any other dimensions to it. This grips us and we are soon subject to the power of our thoughts and emotions, particularly the ones of wanting things and situations and experiences; of trying to hold on to what we like; and of rejecting and perhaps hurting those things we don't want. These are the self-made walls within which we live a rather dreary and often a suffering life. It has its superficial pleasures but there is no deep happiness. A lot of people appear to live like that all their lives.

But also some say: this can't be all. And as soon as we say it, it's as though there's a response from somewhere, as though just the question seems to move us deeply. And then perhaps we start to look for new truths and new insights. And that's where this boy is, he's begun to look. He's realized the ox is missing – which is the first big step. But he doesn't know where to look or how. For him the mountain is steep and the path is covered over with grass and although he walks round day and night he can't find anything at all and his effort seems all in vain. He's really at a loss what to do. There are many of us like that, having some difficulty in finding a starting point, a teaching which will set us on our way or even – and this would be very convenient – take us all the way. But since we don't know what the way is, we're vulnerable and easily misled – especially among some of the beliefs of today. Albert Einstein once wrote:

> A human being is a part of the whole called by us universe, a part limited in time and space. He experiences himself, his thoughts and feelings as something separated from the rest, a kind of optical delusion of his consciousness. This delusion is a kind of prison for us, restricting us to our personal desires and to affection for a few persons nearest us. Our task must be to free ourselves from this prison by widening our circle of compassion to embrace all living creatures and the whole of nature in its beauty.

> *Ideas and Opinions*

In the second picture the boy has begun to realize where he is
and what he's doing. He doesn't just wander round any
more, he takes stock, he pays attention. It's the old invaluable
exercise of attention again. As soon as we pay attention to
something we become much more aware of it, we're able to
have a relationship with it. A lot of our day is spent paying
very little attention because we're so caught up in our
thoughts and feelings that there's very little relationship to
the real world. But on the occasions when we do pay some
attention we find ourselves in a much clearer world. Such a
change of attention can almost seem like a change of
consciousness. It's certainly a change of direction within
ourselves, from the self-centred self caught up in its own
world to the open awareness of the real world. The self has to

go into the background a bit when we turn our attention onto something else. And it usually has instant rewards. In this case the boy sees a small clearing in the woods and there are the footprints of the ox. He gives a cry of joy. Now he can believe in his direction. And now he knows that the ox is there somewhere, it exists, it is not just a forlorn dream.

There is a mystery here for all of us. The true reality exists and when we want it sufficiently it makes itself known to us. We don't know how this happens, we are given a gift of unbelievable wonder, but there can never be any doubting it when it occurs – and I'm quite convinced it happens to everyone. A lot of people may not want it, others may have a temporary recognition and then go back to their lives,

basically unaffected. And yet others see the traces and rejoice in such a way that there is no going back.

The boy has recognized the footsteps and in the third picture he has followed them for a very long way and can actually see the tail of the ox. For us this means that when we have established the direction to go we then have to work, perhaps for a long time, at removing the obstacles which prevent us getting there. What are the obstacles? They are all really contained in one, and that is the immense and obtrusive sense of self which we have on all occasions and which prevents us letting go and being nothing.

Because that's what all the years of searching, all the hours of meditation and inner looking are really about – the total letting go of self in order that one can know that which transcends self. Such transcendence is beyond speech and intellect and if we try to describe it or relate to it as if it were an object we lose it. To think of it as an object, as separate from oneself, is to deny the true consciousness of no subject and no object. That's why the name God is so difficult to use because for many people God is a separate object. Simone Weil said once that when the world is empty of God it is God and that is the mystery of mysteries wherein we are safe. Plotinus said:

> There are not two: the beholder is one with the beheld. It is not a vision understood but a unity apprehended. This is why the vision baffles telling. We cannot detach the supreme to state it. If we have seen something thus detached, we have failed of the supreme, which is to be known only as one with ourselves.
>
> *The Philosophy of Plotinus*

Echoing this, a Zen master said: 'Should you desire immediate knowledge of reality, all that can be said is 'No duality!' When there is no duality, all things are one, there is nothing that is not included.'

And we ourselves may for a minute, a flash, be so held and gripped by beauty – the sea, the moonlight, a starry sky – that we experience an instant without self, without duality, and feel its wonder and clarity. And that's when we see the tail of the ox.

Now we've seen what we're looking for with our own

eyes, with our own experience. We've walked into the
sunlight, like the boy in this fourth picture, and found the
whole ox. But finding isn't keeping. The ox may drift away
again into the bushes. Our moment when we are without self
and begin to experience the numinous, the wonder of
existence, may never return. So we do what the boy does. He
puts a rope round the ox so as to make sure he's got it and the
ox is rejecting this rope and giving him a lot of trouble,
kicking at him and jumping away.

What is the rope we tie around our insight? It's made up of
intellect and concept. A moment's true experience gives rise
to a whole tower block of theory and reasoning. We think
we're capturing the ox by understanding it with our minds.
We listen to what other people have to say about it, we read,

we compare and check and learn the names. 'That is what it was like, therefore I must have had kensho, or received grace.' But the more we compare it with what we know and what we can name the more the true experience, like the ox, kicks and jumps and won't be pinned down. It's unique, it can't be compared, there's nothing to compare it to. And as for the naming, how can you name it? There is no name that applies. But we all do seem to go through that stage of trying to fit the experience into something that is already known – a tradition, religion or New Age movement. And in so doing it gives us a lot of trouble. In fact it often seems to go away altogether.

In the fifth picture the boy is leading the ox down the road with a loose rein. We are told that it has taken a lot of time to herd it and it still needs a good deal of attention, but it's now more meek and faithful to him.

What does that mean? A long time has passed, the text tells us. This surely means that the truth has to be lived with for a long time before all those intellectual concepts die away and we realize that it has never been separate from us, that it was there all the time, that we are it and it is us. During that long time, perhaps years, we have however remained faithful to our commitment, we have never really given up, although there might have been gaps. We have remained steadfast in our longing and have not been content with lesser satisfactions.

When I say lesser satisfactions, I really mean that there are lots of blind alleys on the path which appear to give insights and genuinely do, up to a point, but which really serve our emotional side, our wish for excitement and drama in our lives. Crystal gazing, UFOs, ley lines, King Arthur and the Holy Grail, they all have at some point an enlarging effect but they can be an entanglement and prevent one from looking for that which has no name.

So at last, when we've been through quite a lot of self-discipline, which for many people may have taken the form of years of meditation or contemplation, we are now at ease with the ox and have begun to realize that he was never separate. He ambles along with us and we don't have to clutch at the rein.

Now the boy has truly caught the ox he does not have to stay in the woods any longer. The sixth picture shows us the ox very obedient and the boy riding its back. He plays the flute on his way home. The boy and the ox are one in harmony.

We could say that for us this means the disappearance of outer forms of religion, which are the woods. We have explored the woods by reading all the books and visiting the teachers and obeying the precepts because we are told to, and meditating in a certain form. But now all this, all the concepts we have examined, can be left behind because we're heading home. The trees of the wood are really all the words of others.

There comes a time when it is essential to let go of all we have heard and believed. The best teacher in the world must not be clung to even if he or she is the biggest tree in the wood. The protection of the branches must be left behind. The experience of just being where you are in the present moment must become the next step and sometimes it needs a lot of courage to take that step.

But once taken, it all becomes surprisingly clear and easy. Everyday life is seen as the greatest teacher, the most satisfying temple for practice, the unlimited arena for all our discoveries. And so we feel at one with the ox, with our pure original nature. But yet – the ox is still there, it is still in the picture. There is still some idea with us of something to be got. There still has to be an ox in our lives, and we still think

of that ox, our original nature, as in some way separate from ourselves, even if the two of us are one.

In the seventh picture, the boy reaches home. And when he gets there he notices the ox has gone. But he is completely unconcerned. He feels no need to catch it again because he realizes now that it is not other than himself. He is at last at home in himself and the ox is no longer separate. This is a totally different picture from the earlier ones when the ox had not yet been discovered. So he is not searching any more, the ox is within him.

But – he himself is still in the picture. He is meant to be rather tiny here in a large landscape, because he has diminished his ego. He is no longer at the mercy of his emotions and thoughts, his actions have become harmonious and clear and his equilibrium is excellent. And the landscape is wonderfully large and spacious, not tightly up against him as it was at the beginning but flowing outwards in all directions. And yet – he is still within the picture. And he is still there because he has a concept that he has reached his goal, he has a sense of attainment. He himself has done it – and that thought keeps him from becoming nothing. And too he still believes that there is a goal, an ultimate state of being to be be attained.

A Zen story tells us that once there was a great judo master who after many years gave the highest honour, his transmission of teaching, to his senior student. He said: 'Now you will teach and I will remain in the office and if you need me sometimes I will come out and help you.'

All the students had a great celebration that night and drank a lot of rice wine in the town and after some hours the new head teacher led them back to the monastery. They were very merry and not paying much attention and they came up behind a mule that was standing in the street. The mule kicked at the new teacher and he did a spectacular roll right over the end of the mule and landed on his feet.

The students all shouted, 'Wonderful! We never saw our old teacher do anything so incredible.' And the next morning they told the old teacher how wise he had been to pass on his transmission to his senior student. But when he heard the story the old master stripped the designation from the head teacher's uniform and said, 'You're not ready to be a teacher, you must become a student again.'

No one understood why he did this, so he said, 'Come with me and I'll show you the correct action with a mule.' He led the students down the street until he found the mule. Then he walked around it about a metre away and continued quietly down the street. Then his students understood. If one really pays attention, is really awake, then one does not provoke some unnecessary thing like violence or anger. A mule has an automatic reaction – if it is startled or angry, it kicks out at whoever has scared it. And everywhere in the world we see the same thing. Automatic reactions, knee-jerks, on the part of politicians, big crowds, footballers – we all have them. But the person who has come to see clearly into her or his own reactions, does not evoke them in others out of carelessness, but sees each situation calmly and compassionately, using skilful means to avoid a harmful confrontation.

So the student who had unnecessarily brought out anger in the mule and then saved himself in a spectacular way, again with no thought for the mule – for the other – was rightly reprimanded by his teacher. He was celebrating his attainment and while we think we've attained something, that we're special in some way, then we can't be nothing, we are still very much in the picture.

In the eighth picture, now at last the boy too has gone from it and it's just an empty circle, the circle that has been the frame for the first seven pictures. Pictures three to seven

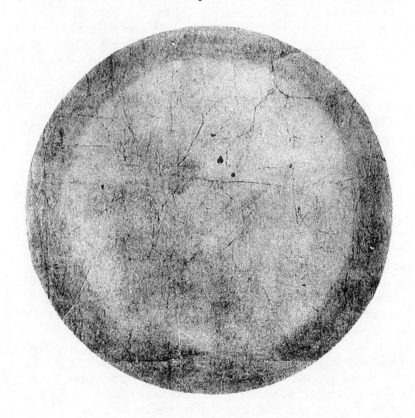

are all concerned with the realm of the conceptual, the making-thoughts person. But in this picture there is no subject and no object, the boy and the ox have both disappeared. There is no idea though of negating the existence of the ox and the boy. When the duality of me here and everything else there dissolves it *seems* as though there is no subject and no object. It is not that they disappear but they are not seen in a separated way. As in my own 'note of music' experience, a different level of consciousness seems to come into being and it's as though one sees with a new eye, an enlightened eye. Then the real nothingness, the real emptiness of personhood is found. But this is not quite the final goal yet.

In the ninth picture some clouds are passing by in the sky and a breeze ripples the surface of the pond. Plum buds are beautifully open. Everything is just as it is. The grass is growing by itself, trees grow upwards and water flows down. This picture means that everything in the universe is already completely expressing its inherent divine nature. When we become empty of delusions and the performing circus of our thoughts and emotions, then our sense organs are capable of revealing the truth to us moment by moment. What we see, hear, smell and touch is the complete truth, nothing is hidden. Buddhism has an excellent word – Suchness – the Suchness of a tree is the essential treeness of a tree; not just seen in a conceptual way but without concepts, as it is. And in this picture all things are appearing just like this, as they are, in their Suchness.

In this ninth stage, the world is seen again and we are back in it. But now it is home and not a foreign country. The poet A.E. Housman once wrote a poem in which he said: 'I, a stranger and afraid in a world I never made' when he was describing his feelings about his life. It seems very true of the beginning of the journey; many of us feel that sense of alienation. But when we reach the ninth stage it's impossible to feel it any more for the world has become alive in a way it never was before. We're not separate from it any more, so there's no longer any existential fear or doubt. We feel ourselves to be whole and integrated and at one with existence. There's a Zen saying that before you begin the journey mountains are mountains and rivers are rivers; after you get an insight into the truth – which is the eighth picture depicting the empty circle – then mountains are no longer mountains and rivers are no longer rivers – the divisions are gone. But when you really come to the abode of rest, which is the ninth picture, mountains are truly mountains and rivers truly rivers.

The final picture shows the last step of the journey. The boy appears again but now he is mature and become a man. He is back in the world, where he is talking to people and living in an ordinary way. He is giving to them without effort – although they may not realize it – all he has learnt because his actions have became spontaneously clear. He is

not attached to results any more and his generosity and compassion are without limit. He is simple and free and his freedom is the freedom from the automatic response for he is able to respond now from the whole of himself. He has come to know himself and to know the unbounded sacred origin of his own nature. So his solitary quest is over and now he is totally at home in the world. He knows he is emptiness and clarity and that he is also form and body and the two are not divided any more. Reginald Blyth says: 'A thing is a nothing but it is also a thing. Forms are no-forms but they are also forms. Everything is the same but everything is different. This is the marvel of our life, the supreme problem of philosophy, and the love of this contradiction makes the world go round.'

This picture, then, portrays true liberation because it shows unimpeded relationship. There is no attachment to self and so there is nothing to prevent us giving ourselves to whatever is asked of us. We are in accord with the Way and at one with the humblest manifestations of existence as well as the wonders because we have discovered that they *are* the wonders.

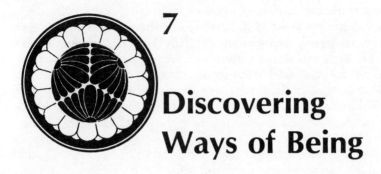

7

Discovering Ways of Being

WHEN I BECAME involved with the practice of Japanese Zen rather than with its theory, I found some difficulties. There are few beliefs more discouraging than the idea that one should sit in a painful position every day, either with legs crossed and ankles on thighs or sitting on one's heels; and that this action should be so controlled that barely a muscle moves, yet at the same time so relaxed that the swinging mind finds its own equilibrium. But many people are sure that such is the right way for them and twentieth century spiritual beliefs, especially Zen, have become associated with sitting in meditation as the main practice. It is almost a heresy to suggest that sitting need not be the one and only way to enlightenment!

Yet this was what I found to be so for myself. I could never quite discover the secret of Zen meditation when eventually I took it up seriously. I learnt that sitting certainly brought about a feeling of being centred, one's centre (somewhere round one's stomach) was a wonderfully strong reliable home. But I didn't have to sit in meditation to discover this, it could be discovered in other ways too, and ways which for me were easier. And other states which people seemed to find in meditation I never could. It was as though the regular times and the static position, and also everybody else's feeling that this was a 'good' thing to do, like going to church, seemed to stifle my natural flow of spiritual feelings and experiences.

So I could not join in the general eulogies about meditation, although that was hard to admit to in the circles I moved in for some years. Somewhat defensively and for my own benefit, I began to note down the ways of being that actually worked for me and during this chapter I would like to explore the possibility that there are other forms of meditation not dependent on an unmoving sitting but which nevertheless do bring a stillness into the soul. They are forms of meditation which grow naturally out of spiritual understanding. They emerge from life itself. They are about enhancing perception, growing into wisdom and flowing into relationship. They do not need such extras as cushions or a shrine room or an image of a deity, but just come about in daily life as one recollects them and mulls them over.

But first, let's have a look at what meditation is aiming at and also what contemplation (a more Christian term) is trying to accomplish. The conventional action for both is to sit still, but while Christians can kneel if they wish and can adopt any sitting position, in Buddhism and particularly in Zen, the sitting position itself is believed to be an aid to enlightenment; consequently much attention is paid to correctness of posture – the straight back, slightly bowed head, hands on knees or together, and so on.

In Zen the main purpose of meditation is awareness. A quiet awareness, without thought or comment, of that which is happening at the moment. Such an awareness brings about the sense of 'no-self' because the barrier between the thinking mind and what is 'out there' diminishes in real awareness and the two become one. Attention to the world in its 'suchness' brings about joy, affirmation and a balanced mind. So through subjectless awareness of events – the body as it breathes, the rain pattering, a dog barking – the events themselves become timeless, sublimely empty.

Contemplation, on the other hand, is a shutting out of all sense impressions as far as this is possible in order to reach intuition of the transcendent. Nobody can explain this better than the unknown medieval author of *The Cloud of Unknowing*. He says:

When you go apart by yourself in solitude, do not think about what you will be doing afterwards, and put away all good thoughts as well as evil ones: and do not pray with words unless you feel you really must. And look that nothing remains in your conscious mind but a naked intent stretching unto God, not clothed in any particular *about* God – but only *that he is as he is* . . . Let that quiet darkness be the whole of your mind and a mirror for you. Think no more about your personality than I bid you do of God's, so that you are oned with him just as you are, without any fragmenting or disturbance of your mind. For he is your beingness, and in him you are what you are, not only because he is the cause and being of all that is, but because he is in you both *your* cause and *your* being. And therefore be aware of God in your contemplation in the same way as you are aware of yourself, and of yourself in the same way you are of God; that he is as he is and you are as you are; so that then your thoughts are not scattered or separated but are oned to him who is the totality.

Perhaps the two ways arrive at the same end – through selfless attention Buddhists reach a state where thoughts and desires no longer dominate the person; and in contemplation Christians find a realm where the boundaries of self have vanished. Both ways mean much dedication and self-discipline. But above all they both imply that there is something 'other' to be discovered beyond the confines of the self. How can it be found?

One of the first things I discovered was that, like the author of the passage above, I needed solitude. No insights came to me when I took part in group meditation – and to be fair to the meditation there was never any suggestion that they should. You meditated in order to meditate and not to gain anything such as an insight. Yet I needed those insights, those moments when my mind became clear and a truth that was right for me to know impressed itself on me – and solitude seemed to be the necessary condition for that.

Which is not to say that I felt anti-social. In every other way to meet with like-minded people and take part in group activities was splendid. It was just in this one, most important, action of discovery of the 'other' that I felt I had to be alone. A lot of my insights came while walking. And although I began this book by describing an experience of new consciousness – well, in a way, that was only the magical kick-off that got me going. During the years that followed I had to make the journey in exactly the same way as everyone else and each insight that arose was both essential and precious.

Perhaps the most necessary illumination was – and is – the action of surrender. I found that when I said to myself 'I want to be nothing' and really meant this, my whole experience of that particular moment became deeper and richer. The colours of wherever I was became more vivid and sounds seemed to have their own strange clarity. Touch too was momentarily full of meaning. I remember once touching a stone wall and feeling that I had never known the rich solidity of stone before. It was as though a new sensitivity grew in me as soon as I could turn away from being my usual self, a self which I came to realize was intolerably full of likes and dislikes and, above all, judgements.

> We live in a world of unreality and dreams. To give up our imaginary position as the centre, to renounce it, not only intellectually but in the imaginative part of our soul, that means to awaken to what is real and eternal, to see the true light and hear the true silence. A transformation then takes place at the very roots of our sensibility, in our immediate reception of sense impressions and psychological impressions. It is a transformation analogous to that which takes place in the dusk of evening on a road, where we suddenly discern as a tree what we had at first sight seen as a stooping man; or where we suddenly recognize as a rustling of leaves what we thought at first was whispering voices. We see the same colours, we hear the same sounds, but not in the same way.
>
> Simone Weil, *Gravity and Grace*

Like a detective, I began tracking down the obstacles to being nothing, to awakening – because it was not often I could manage it – and also the helpful factors which seemed to bring it about. One of the obstacles was my tiresome habit of judgement-making. I seemed to form judgements at once on meeting a person or even seeing them walking down the street. I would be irritated by the way the man coming towards me wanted to walk next to the fence – 'Why can't he step out like a normal person?' Or the young woman with a large dog – 'Why does she make the animal so miserable by bringing it into the crowds?' and so on. One day I got on a bus and suddenly my automatic judgement mechanism switched off. I saw the woman I sat next to as just herself, unique, a fact beyond my judgements, beyond even my thoughts. It was a wonderful experience, profoundly liberating. I saw that the many ways in which people presented themselves – clinging to fences or whatever – *was not my business*. All that was asked of me was to be as warmly skilful as I could in my relationships with these presentations. At the time I noted down: 'It's not my business what other people are like, or what they want from me, or from each other. I think my job must be to accept people and everything else just as they occur.' I found that to see people and events as 'facts' was a help, the very word 'fact' seemed to imply a state of affairs in which there was nothing to be done except adjust myself.

This made me realize what a lot of energy and time I spent trying to alter the events of the day, rather than altering myself. If I accepted burnt toast, for instance, as a 'fact', somehow that took away the irritation I would normally feel and replaced it with a wry admiration of the splendidly black crusts. It did not stop me changing the setting of the toaster but it seemed to make the whole situation easy instead of heavy.

I found that this could be retrospective too. Ever since my day-dreaming teens I had been in the habit of mulling remembered situations over in my mind and altering them to see how they could have turned out differently – better. But if I saw them just as 'facts', then this was how they were, and somehow I need not bother any more about them. It even applied to the long past iniquities of my parents. I had always judged them as deeply imperfect but now saw them more objectively and without self-pity getting in my way, as caring people who could not help failing sometimes, just like the rest of us.

This led me on to the realization that my possessive attitude, my grasp on situations, was a big obstacle. In my desire to surrender and let go I would watch myself sometimes and notice the way my mind gripped what was happening at the moment. It was as though nothing could be allowed to go on in my orbit without my mind taking a firm hold and scrutinizing it, usually to see if it wanted changing for something better, more to my advantage. Again, when I really noticed this – and the first occasion was impatiently waiting for somebody who was habitually late –I vowed to try and let go whenever I could. Vowing doesn't always work but perhaps two times out of ten it will and those times of letting go gave me, and continue to give me, a wonderful sense of emptiness and space.

In my notes, I called this 'everything for itself', and said: 'I seem to be greedy and possessive by nature and I would like everything to be for myself. But when I can really see that possession is a great delusion – that nothing can ever be had – only experienced – and that the attempt at having destroys the experience – then there is true relief at giving up. Once the action has been made – the giving up, the letting go of this minute – then it's as though one has been hiding the sun with one's shadow and now the sun comes out and everything is alive. "Everything for itself" means that it has its own existence, pure and real, no longer the dead outer fringes of my own projected thoughts and feelings.'

As well as helping me to see the 'fact', the woman in the bus had also given me an inkling of what worship was really about. I noted: 'Is it a good corrective against being too caught up in daily life if I tell myself that there is no meaning or purpose in *anything?* This goes against the grain, but how? Is it because I love to make pieces into patterns, to see all the episodes of my life as having point and significance, to see life itself as having some intrinsic meaning? Yes: but if I sweep it all clear by taking the meaning and purpose out of it, I am left with everything existing solely for the sake of existence, and this is incredibly marvellous. This must be where true worship begins, when you see that there is no need for anything at all – but there it is!'

Sometimes a word would lodge itself in my mind and by following the implications of this word I would discover something new. Once such word was 'trust'. I saw that a lot of the actions I was now beginning to take were based on the experience I often had that I was deeply at one with something infinitely greater than myself. More and more I was coming to trust that wonderful infinity, which seemed to be there whenever I allowed it to be. Nothing would induce me to call it God, but I understood Simone Weil when she said that God was in the cracks. I found that when I could make a crack between my busy scheming mind and the world outside I would immediately feel the sensation of that loving emptiness. For instance, if I planned to go out on some excursion and my mind was full of it, if I could just stop and put a space between myself and what I wanted to do – see it properly – then into that space came the thing to be trusted, the right way of doing it, right proportions.

More and more this word trust seemed to be leading me to the experience I was always searching for, of being nothing. And more and more the ordinary terrors of life – accident, injury, death, rejection – seemed to be losing their grip. I felt braver, more able to be a full person. At the same time I sometimes felt filled with extraordinary happiness and it came about for no particular reason that I could see. In the end I decided it was because I felt fulfilled – or, rather, there was a fulfilling going on and the marvellous thing about it was that it seemed limitless. I came to think of religious 'goal' terms such as Nirvana or the Hindu moksha – even such a word as enlightenment – as having no real validity because of their implication that some definite state existed which was the end. The sort of spiritual journey I was embarked on seemed to have no end.

Could death be an end? In the Buddhist circles I moved in death was expected to result in rebirth, but I found such an idea seemed irrelevant. I could not work up feelings for or against it. My sensation of trust was particularly strong when it came to contemplating death and for me it seemed much better to leave it a mystery and trust totally in the loving emptiness to sort it out as it happened. There are now many books on death and dying and as this is a strange century, full of suffering and menace, it is to be expected. But without trust I am sure it is difficult to contemplate death in any real sense.

But whether death was an end or a continuation, it didn't

seem to me to affect the fact that my own job while alive was to keep on trying to become nothing. For a time I was rather bothered by that phrase 'become nothing' because it seemed to have an aura of vacantness, which was the opposite of what I felt. For I noticed that the more I trusted to the emptiness the more of a real person I seemed to become. In the end I decided that 'becoming nothing' was still the best way of putting it, but I ought to know what I really meant by it.

As I struggled to sort it out, I realized that the basis of it meant, oddly enough, relationship. In moments of nothing-ness I felt related to everything about me in such a total way that there was never anything that could be said. It was as though, when I was nothing, everything was free to be itself; and in that freedom there was complete relationship. I could see then that when I usually put a mental hold on something – naming it, judging it (as with the man hugging the walls) – it no longer existed as itself for me and so no relationship could come about. So being nothing didn't mean that I ceased to exist, but that my sense of existence was changed. And the change seemed to linger on a bit even when the moment passed.

Having looked at some of the obstacles to that change, I started to look at what triggered it, the positive actions which could bring it about. There was no particular order but I noted down some things.

A sense of the mystery of the universe seemed to be important. When I was quite a young child I had felt this mystery but in my early adulthood had rejected it – only to come back to it again when I was under deep stress in my mid-thirties. As a child it had manifested itself to me by way of the wind in the tall beech trees, the feeling of soft grass on my body, the clouds blowing across the moon, the sense I had of being within a place of wonder and enchantment. As I grew up, I felt the world was somehow full of meaning which I could not quite capture, although it was very close. I desperately wanted to know this meaning and in my early teens had an intense longing to break through and enter the marvellous world of wind and movement and light, to be one with it. But when I reached fifteen it all became a bit much. In rather prosaic terms, I wrote down:

> When I wheel my bicycle on my way to school through the field behind the orchard, I begin to have strong feelings about the shape of the trees and God. It is always in this field it occurs, especially if the wind is moving their branches. It makes me very happy, as if I belong to something immense, but it also makes me afraid, too. Because of all this feeling I have had to give up God. I have told Him why and also told Him that I will try and believe in Him again in ten years time when I am twenty-five.

But when I was twenty-five the last thing on my mind was God and it was to be another ten years and more after that before the old feeling of the mystery came back to me. But when it did come and after two decades of heavy emotional involvements, it was like water on scorched earth. I had *forgotten* the wonder of the world! And the very act of coming back to it brought such a sense of clarity and joy that I was able to recognize, once more, that this was my way.

And it was not too difficult. I found that when I looked at anything – a tree, a table, a cat – and made the effort to see it as essentially unknowable, unpossessable, as the 'mystery' which I could experience with my being but never fathom with my intellect, this was a helpful action. It seemed to give the perspective of space to my immediate living so that I stopped feeling so tied to results, so caught up in affairs. But beyond that it also gave the sensation of being newly alive in a miraculous world. Everything that my eyes lighted on, everything my hand touched, conveyed the wonder of it.

I discovered that it was easier for me to look at things in this way in order to become empty and nothing than to try and empty myself first. Many mystics suggest an initial self-emptying, letting all images and thoughts go in order that God, or Reality, can fill one. Somehow this didn't work for me, although I struggled for some time to become empty in this way. But I needed the living world to fill me to the exclusion of myself and when I made the effort and allowed it to do so the mystery came into being. Then I not only felt empty but also filled at the same time and the filling was a deep relationship to things just as they are, in their being.

Sometimes I just needed to say 'I want nothing, nothing at all' and at once the magic would be there, the perfection of gravel beneath my feet, the sodden autumn leaves a wonder of shades and patterns. Paying attention to something – anything – but wanting nothing from it seemed one good way in which my consciousness of the world was enriched and deepened. If I could do it at times of stress it was particularly effective for bringing that sense of space and perspective. It was as though I could hand over everything, my whole self, to the object – the tree, the table, the road.

Although this was not difficult to do it was amazingly easy to forget to do. Weeks of active daily living would go past and then a sort of dryness and raspiness in myself would surface, and I would remember and turn with utter relief and thankfulness to the realm of emptiness. There were times, of course, when it didn't work and I would be desolate, wondering if my neglect had obscured it permanently. But this was never so. As long as I took it seriously, went to be by myself and fixed my eyes on something in total surrender to its mystery, the strange marvel of feeling that there was a change in my consciousness would happen.

I discovered that an aid to this was to 'decondition' things. By this I mean that when looking at something, if I dropped my intellectual sense of what it was, I was instantly in relationship with it, as when I was nothing. As soon as I stopped distinguishing it by name (which of course was similar to gripping it with my mind) it became a wonderful arrangement of lines and colours. It wasn't that its named identity disappeared but that this identity was no longer the most important thing about it, whereas in ordinary life it is. Seeing it in this way removed all sense that I had to judge or assess it, because value–judgements were irrelevant to the 'fact' of colour and shape.

I found I was able to transfer this 'deconditioning' with advantage to what would ordinarily be judgemental situations. For instance, when I was in a post office queue once I became impatient because somebody was asking a lot of questions at the counter and keeping everyone waiting, and somebody else ahead of me seemed to have gone to sleep and hadn't seen there was a vacancy – and so on. My mind was completely involved in trying to control the situation and there were no cracks for God at all. When I came to and realized this, I tried at once to decondition what was going on and in this case it meant that the situation ceased to revolve around me any more but just existed and was itself, things happened because they were happening, just as grass grows on its own. This left me peaceful and content and although it may not have actively helped anyone else, at least the aggressive atmosphere I was creating changed.

Another help was to try to have no expectations. This sounds dull but the effect is the opposite of dull, in fact it's the expectations we have which are so often dull because they take things for granted. For instance, if one has lived for some years in the same place one almost ceases to look at it because one knows so well what's there. One's expectations become stereotyped. But suppose one is in a foreign country where nothing can be taken for granted – what excited attention one pays to everything! I found that if I could wipe away my sense that I knew everything beforehand I could pay far more attention to what was in front of me; and the very act of attention, as I had already found out, was richly rewarding in a whole range of ways. The action was similar to when I said: 'I want nothing', but in some ways easier to do.

For instance, the simplest things attended to and gazed at seemed to bring a shock of delight – train rails gleaming in the sun, the colours of a traffic light, the glint of water – and this intense delight seemed only to need that one simple act of attention from me. I would give it my full attention and there it would be, the moment of enchantment. I came to realize that usually I never looked at anything properly. Not only did I take it for granted, but my thoughts anyway would be dominating me completely and I a thousand kilometres from the place I was in. Then the traffic lights would be mere traffic lights, only to be observed because they must be and not in any sense something to be looked at for themselves.

Indeed, I found that paying attention was perhaps the key to unlocking a number of doors. Sometimes, instead of making the act of surrender to wherever I was, I would deliberately look at something – a stone, a chair, even my typewriter, it really didn't matter what – and if I could really keep my attention on it in the right way it began to seem as though it was something foreign and vastly fascinating, something I had never seen before. The 'right way' meant not straining, not glaring at the poor thing in an 'I am now attending to you' kind of way, but somehow letting one's eyes rest on the object, lean on it, let it be one's total support. This did not mean 'deconditioning', there was no need to let go of one's knowledge of the thing, but somehow it did mean letting it be itself. I remember looking at the branch of a tree in this way and after about ten minutes I began to notice shadings of light that I had never seen before and the branch and I seemed to be in relationship, as when I was nothing.

So to sum up a little, it seems to me that it is possible without going in for strict meditation sessions to at least set out on a path towards those goals of meditation talked of earlier – the growth of empty awareness and the extension of human boundaries. I discovered much inner happiness this way and I also discovered what relationship, for me, really is – the becoming at one with the present situation in its 'thusness', an unimpeded relationship, a sphere beyond the world of opinion; and the consequent surrender to all things in their sacred beingness.

8

Working Towards Transformation

WHAT MAKES FOR a dedicated life? More and more I was discovering that I *needed* to be at one with things. At the beginning, those fleeting moments of wonder had seemed extra to my everyday existence and it was ordinary life that was important. But as time went by it seemed as though ordinary desires receded a little and the longing for inner space grew.

Most importantly I became convinced – not just with my mind but throughout my whole organism – that something greater than myself existed. I could no longer call it 'other' because it seemed to include the whole of myself. I could certainly not call it God because that name solidified it and turned it into an object at once. What it really seemed to be was a dimension of being. And in a way it was still 'other' because I felt it was always there, never absent, whereas I was by no means so faithful in choosing to be aware of it.

When I was aware of it, though, it turned the whole world into a gift. Not to be possessed, but to be experienced. The rainy sky was a gift, the newspaper boy cycling up the road was a gift – as soon as I could see everything as a gift in this way I could relish it and relate to it. So awareness of that other dimension of being was something I wanted very much to cultivate. But how?

In the last chapter I described some of the ways that evolved as I got to know existence and to know myself at a deeper level. But they did not all arrive at once and in the meantime I searched for some guidance in the religious scenery of the sixties and seventies, when a lot of my discoveries took place.

I continued to love the old Chinese masters, who obviously knew exactly what I was discovering. And I was also very attracted to Buddhism, it seemed so clear and sane. When I came to know it better I found of course that quite a lot of 'religiosity' was there too, but even so its basic tenet that one should find out the truth for oneself seemed to me the right way.

But one thing bothered me about Buddhism. In the school called the Theravada, which was supposed to convey the basic teaching, there was much talk about seeing into the true nature of existence and this meant denying that there was any sort of a self; or if you still thought you had one, you were to get rid of it by analysing the constituents of which it was made up – feelings, consciousness and so on –· and seeing that no self could reside in any one of those.

To get rid of the self was not, to me, the same as becoming nothing. In becoming nothing there was no denial of the self, only the feeling that it had been eclipsed for something greater. But Buddhism had this bothersome obsession with denying the *existence* of the self. It insisted that there never was such a thing from the beginning. And yet all my discoveries were about that state of being which was both other and also my 'self'. Not only that, but there was the sense of something extraordinarily personal at various times that I could not possibly want to do away with. For instance, a number of times I had felt myself to be deeply loved. It was to do with the trusting. It seemed that as I trusted so I was, in some strange way, received – and this felt like tender love. Once, too, when I was feeling rather lonely and hard done by I seemed to be enveloped in comforting compassion. If the personality did not exist then none of these things could exist either and I could not agree to that, nothing would induce me to deny their validity.

One of the people who came to my rescue over the Buddhism versus personality conundrum was Alan Watts. He was a philosopher who, at the age of sixteen, had written a book on Zen which is still in print today, over fifty years later. He had a keen wit and great gifts of putting difficult concepts into easy language. His spiritual home was in Zen (he was delighted when he was invited to Japan to teach it to the Japanese) and in the conversations we had and in his books I found I was able to bring the Buddhist no-self idea and the deep self experiences into some harmony.

He suggested that the idea of no-self really meant no permanent self. Even the Buddha had acknowledged a *sense* of self but declared, on examination, that everything about it was conditioned and subject to birth and death and thus it was only relatively and not ultimately real. According to Alan, to believe that one's self, that 'me', was a fixed, permanent reality – which we all tend to do – leads to a sense of isolation from the rest of the world and consequent 'hostility and plundering expeditions against life'. He pointed out that Theravada Buddhism differed fundamentally from the larger school, Mahayana (which includes Zen), about the nature of the self. Because the Buddha denied the existence of any permanent or 'real' self, the Theravadans take this to mean there is no self at all. Mahayana, on the other hand, considers that the *true* self is found when the delusion of that 'permanent' me is seen through. Theravada is content with conceiving enlightenment as merely the negative under-standing that all things are without real self, but Mahayana completes this denial with an affirmation – that enlightenment is to realize that the self is not 'this person called "I" as distinct from that person called "You", but that it is both "I" and "You" and everything else included'.

I found this helpful to consider because if I accepted that my sense of self was a gift, in the way I had seen my surroundings as a gift – again, not possessing 'myself', only experiencing the feeling – then all the heaviness of being 'me' lifted and a sort of joyous humour about the whole situation came into being. The loving and the comfort I had received were still a mystery but the self that had received the loving was simply part of the mystery too and not to be seen as separate from it.

Yet although I could resolve the conflict in practice, the explanation, even Alan's, did not quite satisfy me. I felt there was an area of confusion here – just as I had felt it with

Ramana and Dhiravamsa. I could still find nothing intrinsically *wrong* in being 'me' (except of course the automatic knee-jerk reactions that one has to grow out of). There was an obstinacy in me which I could not extinguish, that made me believe that being 'me' *mattered* – so although it seemed ludicrous to deny the deep wisdom of eastern religions yet on this issue I had to do so. And it was here, oddly enough, that quantum physics – an area of learning which normally I would never dream of trying to understand – came to my aid.

I had of course been intensely interested in the new thought about physics, with its espousal of Buddhism as conveying philosophically what it was describing in physical terms. I had resonated with many others to Fritjof Capra's statements, such as:

> Particles are not things but interconnections between things; and these things are interconnections between other things, and so on. Thus quantum theory reveals the basic oneness of the universe . . . things and phenomena are perceived as being different manifestations of the same reality. The division of the world into separate objects, though useful and practical on the everyday level, is seen as an illusion . . . quantum theory forces us to see the universe not as a collection of physical objects, but rather as a complicated web of relations between the various parts of a unified whole.
>
> *The Tao of Physics*

So far, so very good; and it was tremendous to feel it was now established that one was part of a miraculous universe. That if one lived properly in it one could be of use to the whole world through that amazing web of interexistence. But once more I still felt that the total picture was somehow not there; that again, as in Buddhism, the personality with all its quirks and oddities had been dismissed as non-existent. It seemed as though it was always glossed over because it didn't fit in with a certain way of explaining the world.

But then I came across the work of Danah Zohar, a physicist, who pointed out that Capra and others were only describing half the reality. All particles have two functions, one a 'being itself' function and the other a wave, or 'relational with others' function. The Buddhist-oriented physicists (and perhaps the Buddha too?) were talking only of the wave function, according to her:

> Particles do exist and so do selves.
>
> *The Quantum Self*

She saw particles not as unchanging or solid but as continually forming new sub-selves in the same way that we absorb new experiences and are changed by them.

> The selves within selves of the quantum person undulate and overlap, sometimes more, sometimes less . . . and their region of overlap at any one moment accounts for the sense of 'I' at that moment. 'I' am all my many sub-unities. This is the most basic definition of the self at any given moment – the most highly integrated unity of all my many sub-unities.
>
> *Ibid*

She makes it very clear – and this was what mattered to me – that because of the quantum nature of consciousness and the relational joining of the many sub-selves (for instance, the hurt-child self, the rebellious self) –

> . . . this shifting, composite 'I' is not nothing, it is not an illusion. It can never be reduced to a mere collection of separate selves nor to a collection of separate brain states . . . Quantum systems can't be reduced in that way. The unity of the quantum self is a substantial unity, a thing in itself which exists in its own right . . . The 'I' and the 'we' is not a case of either/or but of both/and. I am uniquely me, something in myself that only I can be, and I am also my relationships with others . . .
>
> *Ibid*

This really satisfied me at last. I had started to think it was beyond logic, the sense I had that I was utterly of the world, made of its materials, and yet at the same time unique. But the way quantum physics lies at the root of consciousness (its principles are the same, according to Zohar) confirmed at a deep level my own innate feelings that being 'me' was part of the true nature of things.

I found too that I was not alone in this. Frederick Franck says:

> How I have found fault with that poor ego! As if it were only to be despised and to be annihilated at once. As if it were not

an indispensable part of my life-process, that primeval narcissistic ruthlessness needed for growing up, for survival, that I share with ducklings and dogs. Zen does not bid me destroy ego, but to see into ego, into its relative reality . . . Until in the end you see that ego does not have to be cast out but to know its place, until it is 'expanded to embrace all', as Suzuki says; until ego and egolessness live at peace together.

The Zen of Seeing

In his clear way, Alan Watts also understood the importance of not struggling to get rid of the feeling of self:

Total change is the attainment of a true sense of proportion wherein the individual has regard, neither for the universal alone, nor for the particular alone, but for both, for identity at the same time as diversity. And in the realization of his uniqueness he must express that uniqueness to its fullest extent so that its function may be fulfilled, while that uniqueness cannot be truly unique unless he has also the realization of his identity with the Centre . . . '

The Modern Mystic

All the cogitating on particles and waves brought me to realize a truth I had not looked at before. In Buddhist countries the whole culture is orientated towards the community at large rather than the individual. This has always been difficult for us to understand, it is so different from our individual-orientated western civilisation. The Buddha's teaching of no-self and the culture of Buddhist countries are inextricably mixed, so that it is natural for eastern Buddhists to think in 'wave-relationship' terms, not emphasizing the particle at all. But equally it is natural for westerners to relate to the particle rather than the wave, which is what our culture teaches us.

The best way to live, then, would be to balance the wave and the particle and to integrate them, and this I determined to try to do. But quantum understanding helped explain to me why so many western Buddhists eagerly adopted the wave nature of things and tried to ignore the particle – it did not accord with their new-found philosophy. Also it is true we have overdone the particle side in the West and badly need to see our wave nature, so perhaps it is natural to over-emphasize it.

When I met Joanna Macy, a foremost Buddhist, she told me she too had found Buddhism difficult not because of the dismissal of self – although that did matter – but because of (what to her mattered more than self) the lack of the feeling of God. She said:

> It was a struggle, even a conflict for me in my early years of Buddhism to accept that the presence of God was not there. I would sit in practice and I would find tremendous rewards from the practice that were world-shattering, that made all the Buddhist teaching and doctrines real. But still there was not that feeling of being sustained and of being held – that *encounter*. That personness.

She had understood personality in a different way from me – rather more positively – and had managed to integrate it with Buddhism:

> I knew that the nature of reality – that is of such reality, such thereness, such splendour that it could illumine and redeem life and could make sense of my experience of ecstasy – had to be more than my mind in every respect. And since my mind has personality and intelligence and love, then it must include all that too and be not merely a principle but also personality in a much larger sense. I clearly didn't invent being a person. There is a personness writ large of which I am a small reflection. So when I was meditating, sometimes I would shift gears and sit in worship.
>
> Because there was the worship part also. The standing or sitting in *adoration* – I think that is a fundamental posture of the spirit which the spirit hungers and thirsts for. Praise and adoration goes beyond being good and being of service.
>
> So I missed that in the Dharma. But I shifted gear while I sat and so worked on that and chewed it and digested it that it has served me as my koan for twenty years. That sense of *presence* – it's come back to me now through these other ways of constellating it for myself.

Going through some of the same experiences as Joanna – the encounter with the 'other' when I became nothing and stopped being centred in my ego, the sense of 'presence' which had always come to me, even as a young child, in solitary places – I now began to see these as part of a sublime

whole. And too, like Joanna, I came to think of Buddhism as
the right way for me, and in Buddhism particularly Zen.

What I found in Zen (as I had found it in Taoism) was a
complete acceptance of the feeling of the numinous as an
essential state of being. Many of the 'difficult' and eliptical
koans were to jerk the mind out of its fixed ruts and into that
state. And having reached that state, Zen went on to ensure
that a person functioned properly in the world, bringing
what had been experienced into everyday situations, as in the
Ox-herding pictures. The liveliness and practicality of the
old Chinese and Japanese teachers, their freedom and earthy
humour, contrasted well with the tendency to piety of the
Theravada Buddhists.

So what I read and what I experienced both drew me to
Zen. But then I came up against a barrier I had not thought of
– the masters!

Theravada was properly free of personality cults. It could
be that the sermons of some monks were a bit easier to listen
to than others, but that was as far as it went. But when I came
to practise Zen, I discovered to my dismay that a guru
system was not only in place but was much tighter than in
any of the other schools. What seemed to have happened was
that the early Chinese teachers (up to the thirteenth century)
had certainly had their own monasteries yet they had
encouraged their monks and nuns to go from one to another,
because the whole truth could not reside in just one teacher.
But when Zen died out in China and the Japanese took it over
they developed it in a more organized and precise way.
Somehow Zen even sounds more efficient and precise than
the softer Ch'an.

The Japanese adopted the system of abbots but turned
them into masters with a strong, and to my mind rigid,
insistence that their pupils stay with one master – at least that
is what it is like today, perhaps at the beginning they were
more flexible. So in order to really learn to meditate and to
set forth on the Zen path one has to go to a master, called a
roshi (meaning learned teacher) and be accepted by him (or
her – there are some women roshis these days). There then
should follow some years of quite arduous training with a
great deal of sitting meditation and straight backs.

Perhaps luckily for me there were no roshis in England when I first met Alan Watts and found myself so attracted to Zen, so the problem did not arise immediately. I went as often as I could to the Buddhist Society premises in London and 'meditated' with Christmas Humphreys, an unusual High Court judge who had espoused Buddhism as a young man and 'taught' Zen in ways that were entirely his own. And it was all pleasant and quite fun and nothing to do with any real insights but gave me a feeling of being in touch with others who were groping their way towards some sort of realization – I had been lonely from that point of view up till then.

But then the first Japanese roshi arrived and I had several interviews with him and was told afterwards that a certificate of satori (enlightenment) had been issued for me in Kyoto. I had just started a small Buddhist bookshop and wished I had it to pin up on the wall to attract customers because it certainly seemed a silly enough idea. But that roshi did not stay in England and I was free again to maunder on in the Buddhist Society. In fact no roshi has stayed for long in England, as though the English spirit is not really welcoming to a master-pupil system.

But time caught up with me. The Japanese roshis started to go to America and after a time came over to Europe to form branches. So then the question began to arise – 'Who is your master?' and when I said, 'No one', meaning that nobody had yet come along with whom I wanted to be in that relationship, there was obvious disapproval. By that time I had started writing and even written a popular book on Zen, so not to have a master seemed inauthentic and absurd to many people. At that time too a powerful Zen teacher (not a roshi) had arrived back in London after some years in Japan and when I found I could not accommodate to her style, I began to withdraw from Zen. I started to see it, with its rigid rituals and practices, as beginning to take on some of the attributes of a strict institution and I was not prepared to take part in that.

But there were others, I discovered, who felt the same way as I did and who, though more committed than I was to a Zen life, still found the whole master-pupil thing very difficult to cope with. These were American women and they eventually brought up for me the real question of what is spirituality and what is formal religion. For I came to discover that most of what happened in Zen was in the nature of formal religion.

Toni Packer, for instance, was a Zen teacher and the dharma heir to her master, a famous western roshi. She began to question the traditional Japanese forms of Zen. For instance, bowing. Lenore Friedman, writing about Toni, tells us:

> She had learned that bowing can come from a place of selflessness. Prostrating before the altar or before Roshi in dokusan (interview) could happen out of emptiness. But now, when students came to her and bowed to *her*, were they seeing her clearly or putting her above them as an image? And could she be sure that she was not feeling herself thus raised up? What images were created in both their minds? Even though she was wary of – aware of – these things, students might not be.
>
> And what of chanting? There were many chants [usually in Japanese] and they were long and often repeated rapidly several times in succession. What was the purpose of this? If the meaning was important, wouldn't speaking the words more slowly avoid the pitfall of speaking them mechanically, by rote?
>
> *Meetings with Remarkable Women*

Toni was also seriously questioning the harsh and often merciless use of the *keisaku* (hitting stick), with which meditating students were whacked on the shoulders to wake them up and arouse their energy. She was deeply concerned about what the hitting was doing to the minds and bodies of the people being hit. Likewise, what was it doing to those who were wielding the stick? The use of the stick was reverentially referred to as an act of compassion. But did stick-wielding really arise from compassion? And didn't energy awake naturally in the course of self-questioning?

All these queries, and others concerning the wearing of certain garments by privileged students which to my mind led to hierarchy, and also the general master–pupil relationship, bothered me a good deal too. After a certain week of sesshin (sitting meditation) with a pleasant but not altogether inspiring Japanese master, and being hit vigorously by his chosen pupil (I had strong doubts about *his* psychological motives) I finally left the Zen scene – with reluctance, but definitely. Zen had meant a lot to me and I had to adjust myself to the fact that I was not suited to it, at least to the Japanese form of it. So I was left with my original sources of wisdom – the Chinese teachers; and also much Zen literature from Japan by some great but now dead roshis.

Since no other form of Buddhism held such appeal for me, I became a fringe Buddhist. And more of a Buddhist scholar, delving deeper into the principles of Chinese Buddhism, where I still found a great resource of wisdom. It became clearer to me that religion as such, in which I now included Zen, did not express true nothingness; and I was prepared to go on discovering it on my own.

It also brought up for me the whole question of ritual. Since time immemorial people have ritualized worship and supplication and who was I to doubt its efficacy in the light of such evidence? And yet – when I thought about the small rituals which seemed to come naturally to me, they were not really rituals at all because they happened at all sorts of times. I often, for instance, felt the need to bow my head when seeing some wonder – the red and orange sky at sunset, hilltops emerging out of mist, a skipping, happy child. So, too, I often brought my palms together in gratitude for things that happened; and when I entered times of solitary contemplation I would usually tell myself 'let go'. But there wasn't much else of a ritual nature that I found emerged naturally. I could see that if acting in a certain way at a certain time encouraged the everyday world of shopping lists to stop dominating one and a sense of inner waiting and awareness to develop, then it must be the right thing to do. But did ritual, in fact, create those conditions? I thought of Muslim men kneeling five times a day, of Catholics crossing themselves at the sight of a holy statue, of Buddhists taking off their shoes at the door of a shrine room, of the followers of Shiva painting their faces.

How much of it represented a clinging to form, to religious certainties, to a separate deity, to laziness even – a laziness of not bothering to question? I felt that for me the Zen attachment to ritual was one more nail in its coffin. For surely what mattered was feeling love and gratitude and interconnectedness with life and did it really matter how it expressed itself or whether it even expressed itself at all in outward gestures? And indeed why should one action be more reverent than another? Why make a distinction between bowing and lighting incense in the zendo and scrubbing potatoes and driving to work and all the other things we have to do? Why is one action sacred and out of the world and the other, where most of one's energy and time goes, thought of as mundane? Why was it somehow 'better' to cross oneself or bow to the master than, say, to pick up that most delightful of objects, an apple, and bite into it?

It seemed to me that ritual was essentially an expression of dualism, of a God that was not of this world; whereas, if one came to see the world as sacred in itself (which Zen was supposed to proclaim), then the most everyday action when performed in such awareness would be no different from temple actions. Yet I could see there was sense in Alan Watts' assertion that sometimes it is right to conduct a ritual of thanksgiving silently within oneself and other times it is good to 'conduct it in churches and temples with other people, giving it every possible embellishment of music, song and visual beauty'. At the same time, I still could not help feeling that in silence I was at one with things whereas taking part in a ceremony could be emotionally satisfying but was not the same simple thing.

During this Zen phase another difficulty I often heard about was the frustration of women who could not meditate as much as they wanted to because of caring for their young children. The strictness of the meditation sessions meant that no disturbance whatever could be allowed to occur. Some collapsed in tears because they could not get to the zendo and found meditation at home impossible. Others made gigantic efforts:

> It is difficult to get up at 6am to do zazen when I've been awakened four times in the night, and it's nearly impossible to summon the willpower to do it at 10.30 pm when I fall into bed. So what kind of practice do I have? It would be very easy

to give up, except that I have almost a life-or-death feeling about my practice. Without it, I am swept along by events, more or less keeping my nose above water, collecting bruises from unseen rocks. With it, I keep (in small steps) getting more able to meet the moment with a naked soul. The glimpses I get during zazen let me know that it is possible to see through the chaos. The example of my teacher reminds me that it is eminently worth doing. And the mistakes I make with my children, coupled with the world's need for centred, compassionate people with clear vision, remind me that I must keep on. So I don't give up, I do what I can. For some periods I am able to sit every day for 25 minutes; for some periods I sit once a week. Sometimes I feel my awareness is deepening, sometimes I feel I'm sliding back.

This quite typical scenario sounded very frantic to me, not only physically but mentally, as though the woman was struggling to fit herself into some mould that she was convinced was the right one although in fact it might not have been. As far as I could see there was a big separation between a busy life and what was obviously thought of as more valuable, the times of awareness. But would it be possible to relax a little, acknowledge she was not a superperson, and instead try to become more aware of each moment whatever it contained? For then the actual physical feeling of soothing a baby or cutting up carrots could become as centred and 'right' as any moment in a zendo.

Perhaps though that busy mother has voiced a problem that faces us all. It is the problem of finding the time, the desire, the will to become whole to oneself in the midst of earning a living and being a person in the world; of remembering the whole when the part seems more important; of seeing the mystery of each thing when one has to deal with it in ways that seem to preclude the mystery.

Alan Watts talks about an 'unspeakable world', a world which cannot be spoken about – the mystery. It can be experienced and even conveyed to others, he says, without being able to say exactly what it is. 'We do not know what it is. We only know that it is. To be able to say what it is we must be able to classify it, but obviously the "all" in which the whole multiplicity of things is delineated cannot be classified.'

So our problem seems to be that everyday life is a classified existence and it is only in the terms of name and status – such a partial understanding – that we live it. And the more caught up in the parts we are the more we miss even an inkling of the whole – ' 'Tis ye, 'tis your estrangèd faces, that miss the many-splendour'd thing.' At times the parts submerge us and then, like the mother above, we scramble frantically for something that will bring back the wholeness into our lives, the 'other'. And it is here, when we are at our weakest, that the religions seem to offer the solution and to put a rope into our clutching hands. In accepting the rope we also accept the country to which they will tow us and having accepted that country we do our best to make it our own. But it may not be the right place to live after all. Better perhaps to learn to swim and to swim strongly enough that when we find ground beneath our feet it is our own country we have come to.

But when I first became a Buddhist there were other paths to a more whole perspective as well as the religious ones. There was Esalen and the encounter movement, in which people acted out their inner conflicts and thus broke through to a wider vision of themselves; Jungian psychology was at its peak of popularity; Krishnamurti spoke of choiceless awareness and hoped to liberate people from all systems of dogmas and opinions, religions and ideologies by urging them to live fully in the moment without reference to the concepts formed by past conditioning – too hard a task for many; and it was the time too when anything vaguely spiritual became popular and gurus proliferated in every western country.

I was remaining true to Buddhism at that time and was happy in it (it was later that I inched away) but I also found quite a lot of sustenance in Carl Rogers, the humanistic psychologist, and in Abraham Maslow, a Buddhist psychologist.

Carl Rogers had some very sane things to say about the struggle to be real:

> . . . the client moves gradually toward a new type of realization, a dawning recognition that in some sense he

chooses himself. This is not usually any sudden burst of insight – it is a groping, ambivalent, confused and uncertain movement into a new territory. The client begins to realize, 'I am not compelled to be a victim of unknown forces in myself. I am less and less a creature of influences in myself which operate beyond my ken in the realms of the unconscious. I am increasingly the architect of self. I am free to will and choose. I can, through accepting my individuality, my 'isness', become more of my uniqueness, more of my potentiality.

Person to Person: The Problem of Being Human

Abraham Maslow rather won my heart because he talked of the need for what he called 'peak experiences'. In many ways these resembled my own moments of insight and trust and I was particularly pleased to read him during a period of experience-denial in Buddhist circles. It was a phase (probably in reaction to the over-blown claims for ecstasy on the part of many guru-followers) during which some western Buddhist teachers decided to dismiss insight experiences as best not noticed, certainly not made anything of, rather like the embarrassed feelings church-goers have if one of their members talks about visions of Christ. So I read Maslow with some relief, particularly as he was free of the trappings of cult or religion.

Maslow believed that people experience some form of insight every day of their lives. If they learn to recognize it they will be healthier in both mind and body than those who don't because the insight brings not only a rush of vital energy but also of *meaning*.

The meaning inspires the conscious mind with a sense of purpose, and there is no more certain way of ensuring a subsidy of energy from the unconscious than to possess a sense of purpose. This, in turn, guarantees physical health. The Viennese psychiatrist Victor Frankl made a similar discovery when he was in a concentration camp during the war: that the prisoners with a sense of purpose lived longest, while those who surrendered in despair and boredom were most susceptible to illness. For the demoralized prisoners, the unconscious had abandoned its work of 'support'.

Beyond the Occult

To Maslow, the 'unconscious' regions of the mind contained great reserves of beneficent power (perhaps explaining my feelings of 'trust') which was a reversal of Freud's belief that the unconscious was a repository of dangerous repressions. During the peak experience that power was recognized by the conscious mind and benefited both mind and body. Maslow called this 'self-actualization', a level at which people positively enjoy life whatever the circumstances. He observed that humans are the only animals who seem to evolve. The mind is meant to flow onwards and outwards. If forced to be still it becomes stagnant and illnesses develop. Another analogy is that of a car whose battery becomes flat if it is not used enough. One could avoid this state by learning to recognize the moments of overflowing delight which consti-tuted the peak experience, and make the effort to bring them about. He offered as a typical example the case of a young mother who was watching her husband and children eating breakfast when she suddenly realized how lucky she was and experienced a moment of bliss. When she no longer took them for granted but really saw them, she was filled with delight. As Colin Wilson, a Maslow enthusiast, comments: 'she was suddenly swept away by a surge of energy and she "became free". A moment before she *was* free but took it for granted: now she *became* free. She had *remembered* how much she had to feel delighted and relieved about. Our habitual feeling of unfreedom is a kind of forgetfulness.' And he quotes the philosopher Fichte who said: 'To be free is nothing: to *become* free is heavenly.' (*Beyond the Occult.*)

Maslow was the first psychologist to proclaim peak experiences as self-justifying, carrying their own intrinsic value with them so that for the moment of their existence the person became the whole of Being. He saw the experiences as an end in themselves – good, desirable, delightful and often amusing – yet also sacred, implicit with Absoluteness. He believed that they reflected a Reality independent of the person who was experiencing them – a Reality that persisted beyond the individual human life.

Although I thoroughly agreed with Maslow's recognition that such moments are essential, that they are indeed intimations of Ultimate Reality and that one should bring them about whenever possible, I felt nevertheless that they were perhaps just the first steps to a much greater giving up of self, a much more sublime nothingness. Zen masters, medieval mystics, poets and artists had come to this place of transformation and Maslow, to me, was approaching it but not there. It is expressed clearly by Mark Rutherford:

> One morning when I was in the wood something happened which was nothing less than a transformation of myself and the world, although 'I believed' nothing new. I was looking at a great, spreading, bursting oak. The first tinge from the greenish-yellow buds was just visible. It seemed to be no longer a tree away from me and apart from me. The enclosing barriers of consciousness were removed and the text came into my mind, 'Thou in me and I in Thee'. The distinction of self and not-self was an illusion. I could feel the rising sap; in me also sprang the fountain of life uprushing from its roots, and the joy of its outbreak at the extremity of each twig right up to the summit was my own: that which kept me apart was nothing.

More Pages From A Journal

9

The Revelation of Suchness

I STARTED TO write seriously during the eighties and strangely enough the finished book was not the thing that mattered, although it would be untrue to say I did not get satisfaction from it. But I found the really important thing was to clarify my thoughts, not just superficially but quite deeply. Thinking a thing through was an essential part of discovering new truths and writing was the tool for this purpose. Today there is a movement within religions which tends to downgrade anything 'intellectual' and I find this sad because it can only be based on ignorance of how enlightening the proper use of the intellect can be.

I believe there is a paradox here. When I put an insight into words it seemed to bring it alive and give it power and the potential for growth. But then, after that, I needed to let the words go again. They had done what they were capable of, which was to bring the experience into the light of consciousness, but if I let that be the end of the insight it would die. I found it was essential for the words to come and then to go.

After all, we have been endowed with the human ability to think and to express our thoughts – what ingratitude to assume that this is some sort of fault in the system! Much better surely to make use of it as well as we can. To be able to use words to enlighten is as much a part of the Mystery as any of our other gifts – so long as we are prepared to drop

words when they have done their job and to be wordless and
nameless once more.

But I do believe that laziness – the refusal to delve deep
enough into what it is to be alive – is often a cause of
suffering. We need to know things fully and profoundly and
with all our powers of acknowledgement, for if we don't
acknowledge something properly it passes us by and often
we suffer in consequence.

> Man was made for joy and woe
> And when this we rightly know
> Thro' the world we safely go.
> *William Blake*

So I was happy at that time to find the ways in which the
'other' was expressed – not just to reassure myself, although
some of this might have gone on too – but also to celebrate
and bring into the light what other people had found.
Perhaps it stemmed from some spiritual loneliness on my
part, but I loved to find new ways of describing my own
discoveries, as these ways very often deepened and enriched
my own understanding and helped me become more aware.

One such discovery was the Chinese Buddhist school of
Hua-yen. For years I had been groping after a confirmation
that my 'becoming nothing' was somehow mysteriously
received and reciprocated by all that was around me. In my
childhood it had been the wind that spoke to me of the 'other'
and somehow I wanted to find a similar connection between
myself and all that existed. I wanted an affirmative declaration
that the interconnection and interexistence spoken of in
Buddhism and physics *mattered*, that it was more than a good
philosophy, that one could feel it as a fact. With Hua-yen I
came very close to that feeling.

Fa-tsang, the seventh century founder of Hua-yen, pronounced that because of this interconnected nature of the
universe, it is possible to:

1. Look into the serenity of mind to which all things return;
2. Realize that the world of particulars exists because of the
   One Mind;
3. Observe the perfect and mysterious interpenetration of all
   things;

4. Observe that there is nothing but Suchness;
5. Observe that the mirror of consciousness reflects the images of all things, which thereby do not obstruct each other;
6. Observe that, when one particular object is picked up, all the others are picked up with it.

Hua-yen Buddhism

I became particularly happy with number 4 – 'Observe that there is nothing but Suchness'. Suchness, which I have mentioned before in this book, is for me the essential quality of the numinous. In Buddhist terminology it means seeing the sublime emptiness of each thing and at the same time its particularity in the world, so that its nature as tree or stone or sea-wave is somehow made blazingly real. It is catching a glimpse of its intrinsic nature as whatever it is in itself – person or horse or cat. This was my experience when I was nothing. I found Zen literature abounded in verses and sayings that brought me back to that state.

Haiku in particular was resonant with it. A haiku is a Japanese form of verse consisting of seventeen syllables and said to hold the highest feelings human beings are capable of. It presents us with the object devoid of our mental twisting and emotional coloration. R.H. Blyth, a great collector of haiku, says:

It is a way of returning to nature, to our moon-nature, our cherry-blosssom nature, our falling leaf nature, in short to our true nature. It's a way in which the cold winter rain, the swallows of evening, even the very day in its hotness and the length of the night become truly alive, share in our humanity, speak their own silent and expressive language.

Zen in English Literature and Oriental Classics

Such a haiku is:

A huge firefly
Waveringly
Passes by.

Or:

Among the grasses
An unknown flower
Blooming white.

It seems as though, in those very short statements, a whole world has come into focus because the awareness of it has been total and the eye of the poet has seen it, been gripped by it, and out of that encounter has come the relationship with existence that I always longed to see acknowledged.

I found other bits of confirmation. The Korean master, Ku San, said:

> All beings and all things are not separate from the true-nature. The characteristic of this true-nature is simply 'it is'. And because this nature cannot be added to or taken away from it's the same in all of us. There is not more in a clever person or less in an ordinary person. This nature encompasses limitless space and when you see the perfection of this nature, that seeing purifies your vision. When your visual sense-base is purified then your other senses become purified too and the entire world becomes a pure garden of happiness.
>
> *Nine Mountains*

A 'pure garden of happiness' is not a western way of seeing the world but I knew what he meant. Even more, though, I liked the words of the modern Korean master, Seung Sahn, who said:

> Blue mountain and green woods
> Are our eminent teacher's clear face.
> Do you understand this face?
> *Bone of Space*

I had often thought that for me the visual sense Ku San spoke of was the most important one and that it was because of it that I was able somehow to go beyond it. Although I love much music and many sounds, I could never use my ears in the same way. In the descriptions of Suchness I discovered that I was not alone in finding the eyes to be the gateway to the numinous. For instance, when the Zen master Satcho was asked where the demarcation line is between this world of suffering and the perfection of Nirvana, he answered: 'The eye is the demarcation line' – meaning that the everyday world is Nirvana if it is seen with an awakened eye.

That seems to be one particular way of contemplation – a total surrender to looking. Thomas Merton says: 'Zen explains nothing. It just sees. Sees what? Not an Absolute

Object but Absolute Seeing.' And such a way of seeing is referred to over and over again in Zen literature. When the master is asked, 'What is Reality?' he replies, 'The cypress tree in the courtyard' or 'The bamboo grove at the foot of the hill'. The questioner must wake up to the true nature of the cypress tree, the bamboo – the true nature of the world when it is seen as sacred in its Suchness.

The Zen master Ronan wrote:

> The moon's the same old moon,
> The flowers exactly as they were,
> Yet I've become the thingness
> Of all the things I see.
> *Essays in Zen Buddhism*

And the master Wanshi remarked, 'Just pick up anything you like: in everything it is so nakedly manifested.'

Seeing the wonder gives one the feeling that one is using one's sight for the first time. Until then one had only looked and recognized. But now one sees differently and everything that is there in front of one's eye discloses its Suchness, its mystery. As Flora Courtois says:

> Of all the changes, the one that seemed to me in some mysterious way to be the key to everything else was the change in vision. It was as if some inner eye, some ancient centre of awareness, which extended equally and at once in all directions without limit and which had been there all along had been restored. This inner vision seemed to be anchored in infinity in a way that was detached from immediate sight and yet at the same time had a profound effect on sight.
> *An Experience of Enlightenment*

One should turn away from the label, said Evelyn Underhill when she wrote about her own way of seeing, and surrender oneself to the direct communication which is pouring out of the object.

> Such an experience becomes a feeling of sensation only, without thought. It is the essential sensation, the one the mystics term 'savouring', the one of which our limited bodily senses give us only a fleeting glimpse. In this intimate union, this 'simple seeing', this complete surrender of the soul to the impress of a thing, here at last the sacred powers of sense can

be used fully and properly. And because they are being used, because they are being concentrated upon, because their reports are accepted in simplicity, the result is that the sense-world appears to the meditator as a theophany, an appearance of the divine. Not a symbol, but a showing, which is different.

Mysticism

For me, the whole philosophy of Hua-yen, with its emphasis on Suchness, on 'theophany', rang with meaning. But unless one has first had the experience of seeing the Suchness, it is difficult to grasp Hua-yen. When I first began to tackle it I found an ally, strangely enough, in the writings of Martin Buber, the great Jewish philosopher. The example he uses of how to look at a tree illustrated for me the whole structure of Suchness.

When he contemplated a tree, he said, it might be in one of several ways. He might look at the tree as an artist would, seeing a composition of colours – splashes of green about the pillar of the trunk against a blue and silver background. Or, imaginatively, he might 'feel' the tree in its own movement of veins flowing round the core, of roots sucking from the earth, of leaves breathing in the air, and the whole tree growing of itself in the darkness. Still in the realm of the tree as an object of his perusal, he might observe it botanically as one of a named species. Or he might recognize it as an expression of universal natural laws, and dissolve it into a series of numbers. On each of these occasions the tree would be It, his object, and would have its own place and time span.

But if, 'through will and grace', he was drawn into a relationship with the tree so that it no longer existed outside himself as a separate object – so that the duality of I-it ceased and was replaced by a wholeness of being in which the feeling of separation vanished – then the tree would exist in a different way altogether.

This would not mean that all the other ways of looking at it and descriptions of it were rendered useless.

There is nothing I must not see in order to see, and there is no knowledge that I must forget. Rather is everything, picture and movement, species and instance, law and number included and inseparably fused.

I and Thou

All that belongs to the tree has been gathered into a wholeness in which it exists as its own reality, as 'tree'. He sees it in its isness, in its treeness, as its own being, a state in which no shadow of himself encroaches.

This, then, is Suchness. The observer, the 'I' who observes, is obliterated by the treeness of the tree, although this does not mean that the I loses consciousness of its own existence. I am still here, I am still physically looking at the tree and would not see it if I closed my eyes. But it is not the same I. It is as though I have been wholed, made one; and the myriad feelings and thoughts which usually fill my consciousness have dropped from me and are meaningless. In an unconditioned and infinite way, the tree is then seen by me as more itself than it can ever be seen when I am identified with my selfhood.

The apprehension of the numinous, of Suchness, and all the other ideas of Hua-yen became in time a principal influence on Zen. They contrasted with the Theravada side of Buddhism absolutely – they could almost have been different religions. To Theravadans the attainment of complete realization meant deliverance from the round of birth and death as we know them and the passing of consciousness out of this realm of manifestation. But Chinese religion felt no such pressing need to transcend everyday consciousness. Humans were at one with Tao here and now, did they but know it, and their usual consciousness of the 'ten thousand things' was the working of the Tao. When it first came to China, Buddhism still retained some of the old desire to escape from the ordinary world of physical form; but under Taoist influence it lost this feeling completely and became a world-transforming instead of a world-escaping religion.

Instead of dismissing the concrete world as valueless because nothing in it was ultimate (as Theravada Buddhism tended to do), the Chinese reasoned that if there is no such thing as self-existence because everything exists solely due to a number of conditions – then everything must have value because it is a cause and support for something else. Each thing, however insignificant it may seem to be, must actually be of great value and significance for its contribution to the 'jewelled network' of our mutually conditioned world. This thinking was the basis of Hua-yen and later of Zen. Each thing was seen as arising from and being supported by all the others which are the world, and at the same time being part of a supporting structure for others. Thus the world becomes a marvel of intermingled co-operation. And it was the genius of Hua-yen that it arrived at the radical conclusion that Ultimate Reality cannot be apart from this process; that the transcendent is also the world, so that in the end Ultimate Reality is everything that exists. There can be nothing in the universe not imbued with the sacred.

For me, dualism vanished for ever when I came to Hua-yen. It stated that Ultimate Reality could be found everywhere (as I had discovered for myself) when I really looked – looked from the position of nothing – at anything. This was it. Here it was.

And here too was the basis of all the Zen stories that had delighted and enlightened me. For instance, there was the disciple who asked a master: 'We have to dress and eat every day, and how can we escape from that?'

The master replied, 'We dress, we eat.'

'I don't understand,' said the disciple.

'If you don't understand, put on your clothes and eat your food.'

That seems such an unsatisfactory bit of advice to our ordinary way of thinking. But in fact our imagination is told to come to a full stop so that eating food and putting on clothes can be experienced as they really are, in their total beingness.

> A monk once came to the master Joshu and said:
> 'I have just entered the monastery. Please teach me.'
> Joshu asked, 'Have you eaten your rice porridge?'
> The monk replied: 'I have eaten.'
> Joshu said, 'Then you had better wash your bowl.'
> At that moment the monk was enlightened.
> *Essays in Zen Buddhism*

Joshu was pointing out that Truth is not other than life itself, and that the most insignificant action can be seen in its

Absoluteness when there are no feelings of discrimination between oneself and what is – when one is open enough to act in accordance with Reality.

So the whole of Zen practice (at least in China) was really concerned with letting go of the self, with all its panoply of thinking and imagination, in order that the reality of creation could be experienced. Certainly such a teaching seemed unique among religious practices because it never left the world of ordinary life. Any metaphysical wanderings by students always seemed to be met by a sharp reminder of the present moment so that the mind was never allowed to separate itself from existence. A student who asked a very profound question – at least he obviously thought so – 'If all returns to the One, where does the One return to?' was told, 'The wind is blowing strongly this morning.' This meant, of course, that the One was the wind, as it was all else, and it was only necessary to see or feel the wind to know where the One returned to.

The Zen master Dogen pronounced: 'To learn the way of the Buddha is to learn about oneself. To learn about oneself is to forget oneself. To forget oneself is to be enlightened by everything in the world. To be enlightened by everything is to let fall one's own body and mind.'

I myself wrote at that particular time: 'The spiritual path is never hidden from me. I have only to look, to hear, to touch, to smell and immediately I can sense the mystery – that is, if I am prepared to accept such an ineffable communication. For that acceptance involves putting myself aside in order to wake up to creation as it is, in its reality.'

Perhaps the discovery of Suchness resembles the Christian doctrine of grace. Except that grace somehow seems to be an act of God which cannot be initiated or repeated by the person. I had always found this difficult in the theistic religions, the belief that God and creation are not one and so God's entry into the soul is not certain. I couldn't help preferring the non-theistic view that the mystery of the origin is never absent from creation; that they are one and indivisible; that there is no Being to bestow the gift of grace, or to withhold it, because the gift is already there, ineradicable, waiting only to be discovered, as the sun is there always behind the clouds.

As Alan Watts says:

> In answer to the question 'How shall I find the secret?' Zen points, not to a supernatural Being, but to the life of everyday experience. Instead of asking us to empty ourselves that we may be filled with the grace of a God in whom we may or may not believe, it asks us to make the same sort of relaxation, of 'letting go', to the familiar life in and around us.
>
> *The Way of Zen*

Such letting go means accepting things as they are, which is not always easy. The poet Basho wrote a haiku:

> Fleas, lice,
> The horse pissing
> Near my pillow.

The whole mystery is still there in these things too and if we deny their existence by trying to rid ourselves of them because they seem repellent, we are stifling life itself. However difficult it is, we have to accept their existence. R.H. Blyth, Basho's translator, comments: 'There is to be a feeling of the whole, in which urine and champagne, lice and butterflies take their appointed and necessary place.'

When I used to go to the Buddhist Society, we often chanted the Heart Sutra. A sutra is a scripture (this one was mercifully brief) and the Heart Sutra belongs to Zen and undoubtedly originates in Hua-yen. We chanted it in Japanese, which seemed fairly silly to me even at the time since none of us spoke a word of it, but translations were available and occasionally we chanted it in English too. The most cogent lines were:

> Form is emptiness, and the very emptiness is form; emptiness does not differ from form, form does not differ from emptiness; whatever is form, that is emptiness; whatever is emptiness, that is form.

For my own use I substituted the word 'mystery' for 'emptiness'. But I also felt the emptiness too as a nothingbutness. In a way, only the word 'emptiness' could convey that exact feeling of mystery.

But then I came across a strange effect. If I took it that ultimate reality was expressed in, say, this leaf, that was all right. But if I accepted that there was *nothing but* this leaf, nothing but form to reveal the emptiness, I felt as if I had slammed myself up against a wall because it seemed then as though there was nothing transcendent at all, as though the mystery was for ever pinned down into form. But I was quickly put right. Francis Cook, the exponent of Hua-yen, explained:

> There is a single reality and it is ultimate. Most religions seem to insist that the ultimate reality is transcendent, but if transcendence means in essence different from other beings, Buddhism's ultimate would not seem to be ultimate. However, like Brahman of Hindu Vedanta, the Buddhist ultimate is transcendent in one sense while being immanent at the same time. It is immanent because it is nothing other than what we see before us; nor does it transcend the world either spatially or temporally. However, it is transcendent *qualitatively* as that numinous nature of things which is the object of religious practice and the content of enlightenment. That numinous quality is not just things as *things* but the way in which these things be and become.
>
> *Buddhist-Christian Studies*

And put in even clearer language was a passionate plea for Suchness by one of Iris Murdoch's characters, Father Bernard, in *The Philosopher's Pupil*. He says:

> For what is real and true look at these stones, this bread, the spring of water, those sea waves, this horizon with its pure untroubled line. Only perceive purely and the spiritual and the material world vibrate as one. The power that saves is infinitely simple and infinitely close at hand.

10

The New Spirituality

AS I WRITE this the Gulf War has ended. In the Middle East it has left behind terrible legacies of suffering and hatred and as always one asks the question, what is it within humankind that *wants* destruction, murder, suicide? Why do we kill each other? The terrible injustices of life – the torture people endure in prison camps, the starvation of the poverty-stricken, the build-up of weapons of destruction – it is easy to wonder, as Aldous Huxley did, if this world could be the hell of some other planet.

A Buddhist would answer that we do these things through ignorance of our true nature, and perhaps that is right. It is as though we get carried away by our human passions, suffocated by them, and nothing else is real but the urge of the moment. There is no emptiness, no space, and we ignore or forget the balance and perspective that awareness of space can bring.

But evolution has ensured that this is not the whole story. There are still those who do not lose all perspective and who try to see beyond the immediate moment to the greater issues which still remain.

One such issue, and it is one which I believe may turn out to be the basis of a new spirituality for our time, is that of the plight of the earth itself. Global catastrophe on a scale that the Gulf War couldn't match is not impossible. The gloomy forecasts are being met, though, by efforts among people who want to understand the forces set in motion and try to redeem the situation and heal the earth. The concept of Gaia (the ancient Greek name used by James Lovelock, the scientist, for the living organism which he considers the earth to be) has caught on all over the world and new feelings of relationship and respect for Gaia and the whole universe have come into being.

Such feelings are in essence spiritual. They bring us to look afresh at the amazing beauty of the earth and the stars and planets. If green life is doomed then I want to feel greenness with my whole being before it goes. If water will be polluted then I long to drink its cold purity while I can and gaze into its transparent depths. If the seas are to become dead chemical cesspools (as is forecast for the North Sea) then I must walk along the beach today and revel in the glassy curves of the waves as they break on the shore; stand on the cliff and gaze out over the magic expanse of deepest blue. If the winds are to be dust-filled then I shall treasure now the scented south wind when it comes on a summer's night and listen, as when I was a child, for its message of enchantment.

> What would the world be, once bereft
> Of wet and wildness? Let them be left.
> O let them be left, wildness and wet;
> Long live the weeds and the wilderness yet.
>   Gerard Manley Hopkins

Can we think of a world that isn't green? Green growth is precious in whatever country we live. We have lacked a voice such as Hildegarde of Bingen's (Chapter 3) in our civilization during the time between her century and ours. But now some of that same reverence and adoration for the green and mysterious world – for the numinous which is so near to us – has begun to touch us because, for the first time in history, we can no longer take greenness for granted, the beauty has become fragile and on the point of disappearing for ever.

I believe this is the opportunity for a new spiritual vision, the seeing of our interconnection with all about us – plants, animals, people. Our dependence on them, and theirs on us, shows us the need to cherish what is still here. I am certain we need the environment not only for our physical support but also for our enlightenment – and at least the threat to the world is bringing the wonder and the mystery of existence to the notice of more people than ever before.

Joanna Macy, who teaches ecological spirituality, says:

> In our own time, as we seek to overcome our amnesia and retrieve awareness of our interexistence . . . we open to new spiritual perspectives. We move beyond the dichotomy of sacred and secular. Instead of vesting divinity in a transcendent other-wordly being, we recognize it as immanent in the process of life itself . . . we recognize that, like us, God is dynamic – a verb, not a noun. And in so doing we open to voices long unheard, and to voices that speak in fresh ways of our mutual belonging . . . Thus do we begin again to reconnect. That indeed is the meaning of religion: to bond again, to remember.
>
> *Despair and Personal Power in the Nuclear Age*

Perhaps the new spirituality, the movement towards wholeness and integration, would not be reaching so many people were it not for the almost equally new understanding by physicists of the structure of the world. David Bohm likens the movements of electrons, the basic particles, to those of a dancer responding to a score. The score, the music, is the 'common pool of information that guides each of the dancers as he takes his steps . . . ' The way we see existence has always been conditioned by what the scientists tell us the world is made of. Now it seems to be made of dancing steps and we have to learn to follow the dance.

For a scientist this is a strange state of affairs; and acknowledgement of consciousness in the very atoms that make up the universe is one of the reasons why the ecology movement is edging its way towards a new form of spirituality too. For such an understanding brings about a shift in our whole relationship with the material world. We are now having to realize that we are living in a universe pervaded by consciousness – a dancing universe.

What does such a dance mean, in human terms, for us? I believe it means the recognition of delight, of finding a new world within the known world, of becoming aware of the enchanted essence that lies within appearances.

Delight springs up when we see the ordinary as transparent,

translucent, revealing the Mystery to us if we are ready to enter the colourful, immediate world of here and now with all our being; and are ready at the same time to surrender ourselves totally to the Mystery which lies beyond space and time.

A spirituality of delight is one in which we will often say *'Ah!'* A Zen master once said: 'Have you noticed how the pebbles of the road are polished and pure after the rain? And the flowers? No words can describe them. One can only murmur an "Ah!" of admiration. We should understand the "Ah!" of things.'

'We need nothing but open eyes, to be ravished like the Cherubims,' says Traherne.

To be ravished in this way means we are no longer closed in by our separate selves but are open to the new. It means being ready for this exact moment now, available to all that will happen in it.

Meinrad Craighead, once a nun and now an artist in New Mexico, once told me of that sense of 'Ah!' she felt when she walked in the woods:

> You go for a walk and are with the birds – sometimes you see a coyote out there – and it's as near as you can get to paradise. Which is not to say that I think this world is anything less than paradise. In a way my dreams and fantasies make me cherish the world even more – I cherish every flight of a bird or cry of a hawk or movement of the river at a particular season – and it is one movement, I know that. What I see with my eyes is really no different from what I'm seeing at night or in dreams, or in prayer. It's all one. There are just many levels of experience and I guess that's what it's all about. It's one whole with different levels. But you can't live at any one level all the time.
>
> So that those moments of overwhelming beauty, they're just for an instant. When She moves through your life like that, it's with the same gasp of marvel as when you're out in the woods and you suddenly see – 'oh god, a wolf!' and then it's gone. But just for that second, what you've been given – well, there's no way to measure what you've been given. It really is an epiphany, a manifestation, a visitation and the visitation fills you with such joy and happiness and surprise and humility and gratitude and thanksgiving that when you

don't have it – you are waiting for it and I guess that's what life is, you're waiting for God. But at the same time it's not that you're waiting for something that isn't there.

In some ways the theme of this book has been the 'Ah!' of wonder and delight – the seeing of paradise in the flight of a seagull or the glimpse of a rain-washed pebble. Such a spirituality may seem very slight to many people but I believe it has a long tradition and one which will now enter a new phase as we begin to revalue the earth.

The tradition consists in raising as much of life as we can to the level of a sacrament. I believe that early humans felt themselves in touch with the gods of sun and moon, in touch too with even the timelessness of death. They felt the sacredness of all life, particularly of the animals they hunted. Eating the flesh of the animal was raised by ritual into the realization of the unity between human and beast. There is plenty of evidence to show that all the actions of humanity – eating, drinking, hunting, mating, dying – were all occasions for recognizing the sacred manifesting itself. With sacrament they lifted their individual actions out of the time-bound, meaningless and accidental to a level of significance and timelessness.

It seems that we have never discovered a better way than this to celebrate existence and to join in the dance. To live sacramentally is to cherish and revere everything we see, touch and do.

> The purest acts of worship acknowledging the presence within us are the simple, significant gestures toward the natural objects outside us – touching a stone or tree, drinking water, being with fire or standing in the wind or listening to the birds. Seeing the parts, realizing the whole, connecting inner with outer. The worship is the sensible focus, the will to be still, to receive, to be with the bird or the grass, addressing its otherness, confessing the utterly divine otherness in the perfection of every living creature.
>
> Meinrad Craighead, *The Feminist Mystic*

The sacramental approach to life is one that has not been very noticeable in this century. The psychic shock of two world wars and then of Vietnam and after that of all the other minor wars and bombings, not to speak of the build-up of nuclear and chemical weapons, has created a feeling that we live in a fragile world which at any moment may explode under our feet. For the majority this has led to a reaction of materialistic grasping. But a noticeable minority have felt something else. They have felt that humanity is on the verge of a breakthrough to a different dimension of living. The women's movement, the New Age, the influence of eastern religions, the discovery of American Indian wisdom – all are approaching that different way of being, that bursting into flower, which is essentially sacramental life.

What it demands as its condition for coming into being is that each of us should develop an inner freedom – essential anyway, if we are to act effectively within the world. Inner freedom means freedom from the pressures brought to bear on us all the time by the voices of others. It is freedom *not* to judge, *not* to take part, *not* to be carried away – freedom to *be* loving, to *be* compassionate, to act appropriately and rightly in all circumstances. Such freedom is what the spiritual journey is about. It brings a renewed sense of awareness and awakening that nurtures our own innate wisdom. We all have this innate wisdom and when we have the freedom to realize it, it balances and attunes us, integrating all aspects of our humanity. It transcends the rational, conceptual mind. Inner wisdom is not something to be gained, it is something we open ourselves to; it can't be defined, only experienced.

During the last part of this century, the voices of those who proclaim sacramental life and inner freedom – who declare that daily living is not an end in itself but has to be imbued with a dimension of higher consciousness – have been growing stronger. There have always been some voices, and now there are more, both within religion and outside it.

In Christianity, for instance, Matthew Fox, a Dominican scholar, celebrates a new theology which is creation centred. He says:

> To live is not merely to survive. Living implies beauty, freedom of choice, discipline, celebration. What has been most lacking in society and religion in the west for the past six centuries has been a Via Positiva, a way or path of affirmation,

thanksgiving, ecstasy . . . of life, not death, of awareness, not
numbness, of loving, not control.

Original Blessing

The Via Positiva, he says, is a way of tasting the beauties and
cosmic depths of creation. Without this solid grounding in
creation's powers we become bored, violent people. We
become necrophiliacs in love with death and the powers and
principalities of death. With the Via Positiva all creation
breaks out anew.

Outside Christianity too the growth of the psyche is
towards a new way of living which acknowledges us as an
essential part of something much bigger than ourselves, that
we are not and never could be isolated from the universe; that
our life has meaning and significance because of its interexistence with all else.

But if we are to change, we must outgrow the 'human-is-
a-machine' myth that in the last 300 years has deprived us of
the awe and mystery of our old world myths. Douglas
Harding points out that people once used to think of the sun
and stars and the earth as visible deities, intimately part of the
universe:

> All of this has now, we imagine, been disproved. Instead of a
> universe of concentric spheres, we have a centreless one, a
> cosmic potato instead of a cosmic onion. Instead of an
> aristocratic universe, we have a levelled-down one, whose
> principalities and powers have long ago lost all their influence.
> Instead of awesome star gods and goddesses looking down on
> us, we have so many celestial firecrackers or blast furnaces
> blazing away in the night sky. Instead of a tremendously alive
> universe, we have an inanimate one in which sentient beings,
> lost like the finest of needles in the vastest of haystacks,
> manage to scrape a brief living. Instead of a meaningful
> creation, a proper place for the human race, we have a vast
> expanse of mindless space in which living things are the rarest
> accidents, or anomalies. And, in the last resort, even they are
> accidental collocations of particles.

Resurgence, Issue 136

Such is the present world myth, he believes. That is the way
in which the majority of people see the universe. But to think

that humans are cut off from the rest of existence is suicidal. A species cannot develop apart from the rest of life – it can only grow in 'great interlocking patterns of mutual dependence'. He points out that just as the cells of our muscles are useless – and senseless – without our blood cells, as the shaped tongue of the bee makes no sense without the nectar of the flower, so the more you look at one bit of life the more you have to take into account everything else.

> If, then, we seek the living whole nothing short of the entire network of terrestrial organisms, growing up as one living thing from the start, really deserves such a title. And even this vast spherical organization is not yet a complete organism. This living earth-skin is still far from being self contained – for without rock and water and topsoil and air it is as dead as the least of its parts. In short, nothing less than the whole Earth is genuinely alive.
>
> *Ibid*

To actually *feel* oneself in step with the dance and as part of the living whole earth is to cast off the narrow prison walls of the isolated self for ever – once one has breathed freedom, one will not re-enter the cell.

This is surely the new mysticism of our time – to be at one with our situation as humans and know it in a timeless, sacramental way. And very simple methods can help us at least to feel the freedom of our interconnection with the universe.

The Vietnamese Buddhist monk, Thich Nhat Hahn, tells us:

> When we want to understand something, we cannot just stand outside and observe it. We have to enter deeply into it and be one with it in order to really understand. If we want to understand a person, we have to feel their feelings, suffer their sufferings, and enjoy their joy . . . To comprehend something means to pick it up and be one with it. There is no other way to understand something.
>
> The Buddha recommended that we observe in a penetrating way. He said we should contemplate the body *in* the body, the feelings *in* the feelings, the thoughts *in* the thoughts. Why did he use this kind of repetition? Because you have to enter in order to be one with what you want to observe and to understand. Nuclear scientists are beginning to say this also.

When you enter the world of elementary particles you have to become a participant in order to understand something. You can no longer stand and remain just an observer. Today many scientists prefer the word *participant* to the word observer.

In our effort to understand each other we should do the same. A husband and wife who wish to understand each other have to be in the skin of their partner in order to feel, otherwise they cannot really understand . . . You cannot love someone if you do not understand him or her.

The Heart of Understanding

Joanna Macy has for some years taught ways of meditation for interbeing. One that she uses herself at all times – in trains and buses, or waiting in line at the check-out counter, goes like this:

Let your awareness drop deep, deep within you like a stone, sinking below the level of what words or acts can express . . . Breathe in deep and quiet . . . Open your consciousness to the deep web of relationship that underlies and interweaves all experience, all knowing . . . It is the web of life in which you have taken being and in which you are supported . . . out of that vast web you cannot fall . . . no stupidity or failure, no personal inadequacy, can ever sever you from that living web, for that is what you are . . . and what has brought you into being . . . feel the assurance of that knowledge. Feel the great peace . . . rest in it . . . Out of that great peace, we can venture everything. We can trust. We can act.

Despair and Personal Power in the Nuclear Age

She tells us that this meditation 'charges the idle moment with beauty and discovery. If we see and experience people in this way, it opens us to the sacredness of the moment; and we can extend it to non-humans too, to animals and plants. It is also useful for dealing with people we are tempted to dislike or disregard, for it breaks open our accustomed ways of viewing them. For in doing this exercise we realize that we do not have to be particularly noble or saintlike in order to wake up to the power of our oneness with other beings.'

Joanna speaks for the whole new spirituality when she describes her teaching of 'deep ecology'. It is her vision of the future, of what life could be for all of us:

I call it 'social mysticism'. It is very wonderful to see what results it brings. You see, I love the whole concept of incarnation – that the deity could take form. So I like to play with the Hindu idea that God plays hide and seek. I need to do this particularly with people who present challenges to me. For instance, could God fool me by incarnating in this used car salesman? Could God successfully hide as the postal clerk who's taking for ever? That increases my enjoyment of life a lot.

I asked Joanna how she could play such a game when she reads of rapists and child abusers. She replied that it's hard to play it then:

But the whole idea has now become the basis for group work and in the group even the most awful actions can be looked at in this way. For example, at a recent workshop, I would say: 'be chosen by someone you are having trouble with and *be* that person, whether you have actually met them or not'. And it was deeply moving to me to hear how quickly and accurately and with what beauty these workshop participants could speak. One was an environment official blocking all efforts to control toxic waste, another was putting himself in the psyche of his Nazi father. Each person found it was wonderful to be released from judging – free to identify with someone else, however appalling that person's deeds were.

This to me is the coming into form of something I have ached for and I call it social mysticism. Where the sense of truth and enlargement and release that the mystic finds in the mystical experience can be experienced in ways that bring home our real identity, interconnectedness and *interexistence* with other beings. And I believe that this is the awakening that awaits us now, which is necessary for our survival. This is a form of mystical experience – to move out of oneself, to shift one's sense of self and identity to another. It doesn't have to be God – you can become a tree, and it's beautiful to hear people talking on behalf of a Scotch pine or a redwood or a transplanted eucalyptus. The experience people have is that they are being talked through and that they're in touch with something bigger.

So then this circles around again to the notion of Presence. You have a sense of being worked through, of something working through you. And then the workshop becomes a centre of spiritual practice because it's confirming, steadying and challenging. We can find grace this way, it is an earth-created spirituality. The grace opens us to that which is beyond the self – and what is beyond the self knows. So there is the Presence and we are being held there and loved. And that experience is within the reach of anybody.

Perhaps we will see the full flowering of this vision in the years to come. Many voices in this century have signposted the way to it. For instance, Alan Watts, who opened the door to Zen for untold numbers of people and let the wind of that uncompromising spirituality blow through western intellectualism. Who analysed our problems and challenged us to see who we are and how we are related to existence:

Our problem is that the power of thought enables us to construct symbols of things apart from the things themselves. This includes the ability to make a symbol, an idea of ourselves apart from ourselves. Because the idea is so much more comprehensible than the reality, the symbol so much more stable than the fact, we learn to identify ourselves with our idea of ourselves. Hence the subjective feeling of a 'self' which 'has' a mind, of an inwardly isolated subject to whom experiences involuntarily happen. With its characteristic emphasis on the concrete, Zen points out that our previous 'self' is just an idea, useful and legitimate enough if seen for what it is, but disastrous if identified with our real nature. The unnatural awkwardness of a certain type of selfconsciousness comes into being when we are aware of conflict or contrast between the idea of ourselves on the one hand, and the immediate, concrete feeling of ourselves, on the other.

When we are no longer identified with the idea of ourselves, the entire relationship between subject and object, knower and known, undergoes a sudden and revolutionary change. It becomes a real relationship, a mutuality in which the subject creates the object just as much as the object creates the subject. The knower no longer feels himself to be independent of the known; the experiencer no longer feels himself to stand apart from the experience . . . it becomes vividly clear that in concrete fact I have no other self than the totality of things of which I am aware.

The Way of Zen

The Indian sage, Krishnamurti, also taught freedom from ideas of self. He did this by showing the necessity to drop the many ways in which we have been conditioned throughout our lives. He asks us to quieten down the conditioned mind so that the storehouse of memories – the way we have been shaped from infancy by our culture, religion and education – merely delivers what is needed for recognition of a present situation but does not take over the person and dictate his reactions. Meditation, he says, is to find out if the brain can become absolutely still. It must not be a forced stillness for this would come from the 'I' who is always eager for pleasurable experiences and who still thinks in terms of 'I and my stillness' as though each were separate experiences. So the brain must never be forced to be quiet, but instead must simply be observed and listened to. The way thoughts are formed, the conditioned memories which come to the surface of the mind, the force of fears or desires as they arise – all these can be observed; and the more clearly every movement is seen the quieter the mind becomes. Not the quietness of sleep but more the soundless action of a strong dynamo which is only heard when there is friction. He believes this quietness can be achieved without great effort:

> You wake up, you look out of the window and say to yourself, 'Oh, awful rain,' or 'It is a marvellous day but too hot' – you have started! So at that moment, when you look out of the window, don't say a word, not suppressing words but simply realizing that by saying, 'What a lovely morning', or 'A horrible day', the brain has started. But if you watch, looking out of the window and not saying a word to yourself – which does not mean you suppress the word – just observing without the activity of the brain rushing in, there you have the clue, there you have the key. When the old brain does not respond, there is a quality of the new brain coming into being. You can observe the mountains, the river, the valleys, the shadows, the lovely trees and the marvellous clouds full of light beyond the mountains – you can look without a word, without comparing.'
>
> *The Impossible Question*

Krishnamurti and Alan Watts speak of seeing through the false identification and conditioned reactions of the self. Sages such as these have been powerful voices in this century. But the new spirituality seems to me to have a slightly different emphasis. It is less about freedom *from* and more about freedom *into*. In freedom *from*, there is the necessity for a constant observation of the fetters holding the self imprisoned. In freedom *into*, the self automatically loses its fetters as it enters into a larger dimension of being.

Carl Jung once made a pungent observation on the way in which people both heal and free themselves:

> All the greatest and most important problems of life are fundamentally insoluble . . . They can never be solved, but only outgrown. This 'outgrowing' proved on further investigation to require a new level of consciousness. Some higher or wider interest appeared on the patient's horizon, and through this broadening of his or her outlook the indissoluble problem lost its urgency. It was not solved logically in its own terms but faded when confronted with a new and stronger life urge.

We feel our bonds falling away each time we respond wholly to beauty, for instance, and know in our response a wonderful completion of ourselves. The artist John Lane says that such response enables us to live fully in the present without attachment to the past and thus to find the Reality of ourselves. And beauty is at this moment here, wherever we are – we only need to surrender ourselves to it.

I believe we have reached a turning point in human existence, where we are reaching *into* and *towards* a new level of consciousness. We are ready to mutate. The new consciousness will be the way of illumination; and the spur to entering it will be the plight of beauty, the plight of the earth itself.

The way of illumination will be the sacramental way of feeling ourselves part of something infinitely wonderful and infinitely mysterious – a dance of the universe which can only be known by entering into it. It will not be the mechanistic goal-orientated world of the past but people will live more like artists creating their lives in harmony with what the world offers.

A daydream, perhaps – but if we don't change ourselves we will be living in a nightmare and of the two I prefer the first. I believe there now is a movement towards what another voice of our day, the philosopher Henryk Skolimowski, calls 'reverential thinking'. He says:

To think reverentially is first of all to recognize human life as of intrinsic value: it is to recognize love as an essential and indispensable modality of human existence: it is to recognize *creative thinking* as an inherent part of human nature: it is to recognize joy as an integral part of our daily living: it is to recognize the brotherhood of all beings as the basis of our new spirituality. Reverential thinking is a vehicle for the restoration of intrinsic values, without which we cannot have a meaningful future of any sort.

Reverential thinking is not a luxury, but is a condition of our sanity and grace. Those who do not think reverentially – at times at least – simply impoverish their existence. Thinking as calculation is one thing; thinking objectively according to the requirements of science is another thing. Thinking reverentially when we behold the universe in its ultimate aspects, and fuse it with our love, and feel unity with it is yet another thing.

The Theatre of the Mind

He outlines three modes of living which are the basic stepping stones towards a new spiritual life:

1. The coming age is to be seen as the age of stewardship: we are here not to govern and exploit but to maintain and creatively transform for the benefit of all beings.

2. The world is to be conceived as a sanctuary. We belong to certain habitats; they do not belong to us. They are the source of our culture and our spiritual sustenance. We must maintain their integrity and sanctity.

3. Knowledge is to be conceived, not as a set of ruthless tools for atomizing nature, but as ever more subtle devices for helping us to maintain our spiritual and physical equilibrium.

Ibid

The spiritual journey is not one that ends at any particular place. The new spirituality if it leads – as it surely must – to new consciousness, will be entering another dimension but not the final one. It is impossible to conceive that there is a finality in a spiritual sense – it is more that there is just the wonder of continuing revelation.

I have spoken occasionally of my own spiritual journey in this book but have never felt it to be different in capacity from anyone else's. How each one of us lives through our situations and grows from them must indeed vary because we are each unique; but because we are all human beings the journey itself has to be the one journey.

And the very obstacles that stand in our way – our socialized conditioning and repression, our selective inattention whereby we screen out those aspects of life which do not accord with our images – even this large blind' area of our lives, this restriction of consciousness, can be accepted as part of the eternal way of things. We are imperfect and somehow there is also a rightness in that fact, as long as we acknowledge and accept it.

> A duck's legs, though short, cannot be lengthened without discomfort to the duck; a crane's legs, though long, cannot be shortened without discomfort to the crane.
>
> *The Complete Works of Chuang Tzu*

Becoming open to the 'ah' of existence; learning however imperfectly to live sacramentally; seeing the life about me as the ineffable appearance of a Mystery beyond fathoming; learning to be still and to receive; surrendering to what is rather than to what I want it to be – and most willingly because it is what it is – these are some of the ways which have helped me and, I believe, many others. If I can put it into one phrase, it is to be struck by wonder. And I hope – and above all I *trust* – that however often I forget to look, yet the wonder and the delight will always and forever bring me back to my senses, to my true clear Sense.

Bibliography

Bancroft, Anne. *The Luminous Vision*, Unwin Hyman Ltd, 1982.
——*Origins of the Sacred*, Penguin, 1987.
——*Twentieth Century Mystics and Sages*, Penguin, 1989.
——*Weavers of Wisdom*, Penguin, 1988.
Berdyaev, N. *Freedom and Spirit*, London, 1935.
Berenson, Bernard. *Sketch for a Self-portrait*, Pantheon Books, 1949.
Blake, William. *Complete Writings*, Oxford University Press, 1966.
——*Poems and Prophecies*, ed. Ernest Rhys, J.M. Dent, 1927.
Blyth, R.H. *Zen in English Literature and Oriental Classics*, Hokusaido Press, 1942.
Bohm, David. *Wholeness and the Implicate Order*, Routledge and Kegan Paul, 1980.
Buber, Martin. *I and Thou*, T. and T. Clark, Edinburgh.
Campbell, J. *Primitive Mythology*, Penguin, 1976.
——*Occidental Mythology*, Penguin, 1976.
Capra, F. *The Tao of Physics*, Penguin, 1975.
Chardin, Teilhard de. *The Divine Milieu*, Collins, London.
Chuang Tzu. *The Complete Works of Chuang Tzu*, trans. Burton Watson, Columbia University Press, 1968.
Cloud of Unknowing, Anon. *The Cloud of Unknowing*, ed. Dom Justin McCann, London, 1924.
Cook, F. *Hua-yen Buddhism*, Pennsylvania State University Press, 1977.
——*Buddhist-Christian Studies, Vol. 9*, University of Hawaii Press, 1989.
Courtois, Flora. *An Experience of Enlightenment*, Theosophical Publishing House, 1986.
Craighead, M. *The Feminist Mystic*, ed. Mary Giles, Crossroad, 1982.
Dames, M. *The Avebury Cycle*, Thames and Hudson, 1980.
——*The Silbury Treasure*, Thames and Hudson, 1981.
Dhiravamsa. *The Way of Non-Attachment*, Turnstone Books, 1975.
Eckhart, Meister. *Meister Eckhart*, trans. Raymond B. Blakney, New York, 1941.

Einstein, Albert. *Ideas and Opinions*, Crown, 1982.

Eliade, Mircea. *Myth and Reality*, Allen and Unwin, 1964.

Fox, Matthew. *Hildegarde of Bingen's Book of Divine Works*, Bear and Co., Inc., 1987.

——*Original Blessing*, Bear and Co., Inc., 1983.

Franck, Frederick. *The Zen of Seeing*. New York, 1985.

Friedman, L. *Meetings with Remarkable Women*, Shambhala, 1987.

Hahn, Thich Nhat. *Being Peace*, Parallax Press, 1987.

——*The Heart of Understanding*, Parallax Press, 1988.

Hallam, Lord Tennyson. *Tennyson: A Memoir*.

Harding, D. *On Having No Head*, Penguin, 1986.

——Extract from *Resurgence*, Issue 136,1989.

Hildegarde of Bingen. *Meditations with Hildegarde of Bingen*, trans. Gabriele Uhlein, Bear and Co., Inc., 1983.

Hopkins, Gerard Manley. *Gerard Manley Hopkins: A Selection of His Poems and Prose* by W.H. Gardner, Penguin, 1956.

Housman, A.E. *Collected Poems*, Jonathan Cape, 1939.

Huang Po. *The Zen Teaching of Huang Po*, trans. John Blofeld, Rider and Co. Ltd., 1958.

Inge, W.R. *The Philosophy of Plotinus*, London, 1918

James, W. *The Varieties of Religious Experience*, Collins, 1960.

John of the Cross. *The Collected Works of John of the Cross* trans. Kieran Kavanaugh, Washington D.C., 1973.

Julian of Norwich. *The Revelations of Divine Love of Julian of Norwich*, ed. James Walsh, London, 1961.

Jung, C.G. Foreword to D.T. Suzuki's 'Introduction to Zen Buddhism' in Bollingen Series XI, Princeton, 1975.

Krishnamurti, J. *The Impossible Question*, Gollancz, 1973.

Kuhn, Herbert. *The Rock Pictures of Europe*, Sidgwick and Jackson, 1966.

Ku San. *Nine Mountains*, Korea, 1976.

Lao Tzu. *Tao Te Ching*, trans Gia-Fu Feng, Wildwood House, 1973.

Lawrence, Brother. *The Practice of the Presence of God*, Mowbray, 1954.

Macy, Joanna. *Despair and Personal Power in the Nuclear Age*, New Society Publishers, 1983.

Mare, Walter de la. *The Burning Glass*, Faber and Faber, 1927.

Maslow, A. *Religions, Values and Peak Experiences*, Penguin, London.

Merton, T. *Bhagavad Gita*, introduction to, Collier Books, 1970.

——*Zen and the Birds of Appetite*, New York, 1968.

Milner, M. *A Life of One's Own*, Penguin, 1955.

Murdoch, Iris. *The Philosopher's Pupil*, Penguin, 1983.

Packer, T. *The Work of This Moment*, Springwater Center, 1987.

Ramana Maharshi. *The Teachings of Ramana Maharshi*, Rider and Co., 1962.

——*Thus Spake Ramana*, India, 1971.

Rogers, Carl, R. *Person to Person: The Problem of Being Human*, Real People Press, 1967.

Rolle, Richard. *The Fire of Love and the Mending of Life*, ed. Frances M.M. Comper, London, 1914.

Rutherford, M. *More Pages From A Journal*, London, 1910.

Seung Sahn. *Bone of Space*, Four Seasons, 1982.

Skolimowski, H. *The Theatre of the Mind*, Theosophical Publishing House, 1984.

Smith, Morton. *Clement of Alexandria and a Secret Gospel of Mark*, Harvard University Press, 1973.

Suzuki, D.T. *Essays in Zen Buddhism*, Luzac and Co., 1927.

Thomas, Gospel of. *The Secret Sayings of Jesus According to the Gospel of Thomas* trans. Robert M. Grant, Fontana Books, 1980.

Thompson, Francis. *Selected Poems*, Garden City Press, 1908.

Traherne, Thomas. *Centuries of Meditation*, Clarendon Press, 1910.

Underhill, Evelyn. *Mysticism*, Methuen, 1960.

Watts, Alan. *The Modern Mystic.* ed. John Snelling and Mark Watts, Element Books Ltd., 1990.

——*This Is It*, Collier Books, 1967.

——*Way of Zen*, Penguin, 1975.

Weil, Simone. *Gravity and Grace*, Routledge and Kegan Paul, 1952.

Wilber, K. *Up From Eden*, Routledge and Kegan Paul, 1981.

Wilson, Colin. *Beyond the Occult*, Bantam, 1988.

Wilson, Ian. *Jesus: The Evidence*, Pan Books, 1985.

Zohar, Danah. *The Quantum Self*, Bloomsbury, 1990.

INDEX